Hazan Family
FAVORITES

G I U L I A N O   H A Z A N

Hazan Family FAVORITES

Beloved Italian
Recipes

FOREWORD BY **MARCELLA HAZAN**

PHOTOGRAPHS BY JOSEPH DE LEO

STEWART, TABORI & CHANG
NEW YORK

PER LA MIA FAMIGLIA

From my grandparents to my children,

I will forever treasure the taste memories shared with you

Published in 2012 by Stewart, Tabori & Chang
An imprint of ABRAMS

Copyright © 2012 Giuliano Hazan
Photographs copyright © 2012 Joseph De Leo

Page 2: Giuliano Hazan at five years old, fishing off Nonno David and Nonna Giulia's dock in Atlantic Beach.

Library of Congress Cataloging-in-Publication Data

Hazan, Giuliano.
Hazan family favorites : beloved Italian recipes / by Giuliano Hazan.
p.   cm.
Includes index.
ISBN 978-1-58479-904-7
1. Cooking, Italian. 2. Cookbooks. I. Title. II. Title: Family favorites.
TX723.H3345 2012
641.5945—dc23   2011018751

Editor: Natalie Kaire
Designer: Danielle Young
Production Manager: Tina Cameron

The text of this book was composed in Andrade and Futura.

Printed and bound in China

10 9 8 7 6 5 4 3 2 1

Stewart, Tabori & Chang books are available at special discounts when purchased in quantity for
premiums and promotions as well as fundraising or educational use. Special editions can also be
created to specification. For details, contact specialsales@abramsbooks.com or the address below.

ABRAMS
THE ART OF BOOKS SINCE 1949
115 West 18th Street
New York, NY 10011
www.abramsbooks.com

Contents

Foreword 8

Introduction 12

Chapter 1
Appetizers, Salads, and Side Dishes 16

Chapter 2
Primi: Soups, Pasta, and Rice 56

Chapter 3
Secondi: Meats and Seafood 102

Chapter 4
Dolci: Desserts 146

Conversion Charts 168

Index 170

Foreword

What fun it would have been had Giuliano been writing cookbooks when his grandparents—Nonna Giulia and Nonno David, Nonna Mary and Nonno Fin—were still around. They certainly would have been amazed, amused, and possibly even flattered by this taste-filled latest of Giuliano's works. With every few turns of the page, they would have been greeted with recipes for dishes that marked the daily unfolding of their lives at the family table.

When I first met my future husband, I thought his background was totally different from mine. Despite the fact that he spoke Italian and had been born in a town only six miles from my own, his parents were Sephardic Jews who had come to Italy from Turkey and who spoke Ladino—an ancient Spanish dialect—at home. Victor had grown up in America; to me, a girl who had lived almost her entire life in a small fishing village on the Adriatic, America might as well have been on another planet. I didn't know what to expect when, after coming to New York, I began to sample the cooking of Victor's mother, Giulia. Surprises awaited me at the Hazan table. Indeed, some of the food was unfamiliar. Yet to my astonishment, there were also dishes that resembled cooking that was uniquely my mother's—and like that of no other family in my town.

My mother and mother-in-law owed the shared features in some of their cooking to a curious intersection of culinary cultures. My mother's people, although anciently from Italy's Le Marche region, had long since been part of an expatriate Italian community that had settled in Syria and Egypt. Victor's parents, who were first cousins, descended from Spanish Jews who had immigrated to Turkey in the fifteenth century. And so, although our backgrounds were ethnically and religiously dissimilar, there were moments at table when those tastes that had been formed in the Middle East converged. My mother and Victor's mother cooked *bamya*—okra—in the same manner, with tomatoes and lemon; they both cooked green beans with tomatoes and onions until they were very soft, so delicious and so unlike the next-to-raw, grassy-tasting, and barely chewable green beans that restaurants have foisted on us. Both Mary and Giulia liked to make roll-ups of thin slices of meat, which would have been lamb until they yielded to Italian taste and switched to veal; they both liked to hollow zucchini and stuff them with meat and rice, or wrap Savoy cabbage leaves around the same mixture. Giulia's mastery of baklavà was beyond any challenge. When my mother came to visit me in New York—she had come alone because Papi, my father, was afraid of flying—Giulia made baklavà for her. My mother, who had a great sweet tooth, had not had baklavà since she left Egypt twenty-five years earlier, and she all but swooned. I have a passion for baklavà myself, and Giulia's was the best I have ever tasted, even better than what I sampled years later in the pastry shops of Istanbul. Without attempting to duplicate his grandmother's baklavà—doubtless an unattainable goal—Giuliano has produced an admirable version of his own here.

David, my father-in-law, viewed the kitchen as exclusively female territory and never entered it. I doubt that in his lifetime he ever so much as picked up a dish towel to wipe something dry. But that is not to say that he contributed nothing to his wife's cooking. He contributed his judgment, which was uncompromising and often severe: "The *bamya* should have been smaller; it is too mature and gummy." "Why didn't you peel the tomatoes for the rice?" "I would have liked more carrots in the stew; they sweeten the taste." Giulia quietly accepted his comments as manifestations of his patriarchal prerogative, but she didn't interpret them as corrections to be acted upon. She continued to cook exactly as she, and she alone, thought best.

Fin, my father, my Papi, allowed my mother to do as she wished in the kitchen, except in the realm of fish, where he took complete charge. When the fishing boats returned to our harbor in the afternoon to unload their catch, Papi was there with his bicycle to get first pick. He would splurge once or twice during the year-end holidays, but otherwise he did not choose the most expensive fish, such as turbot or sole. Papi, who had retired in middle age, had only a modest income from the small farm he owned. He shopped frugally, but he shopped well, choosing varieties that were no less tasty for being humble. He would often bring home what Italians call *pesce azzurro*, fish with blue skin and dark flesh, such as sardines or mackerel. He grilled the sardines, and the appetizing scent and matching flavor of sardines fresh out of the Adriatic and grilled over small wood charcoal have no equal. The mackerel he cooked slowly in an old, blackened, lopsided skillet, with olive oil, garlic, and rosemary. In Florida, where I now live, mackerel is plentiful, and I have tried to duplicate that dish, with middling success. The Adriatic mackerel—*sgombro*, we call it—is smaller, and its flavor is sweeter and at the same time more intense. When Papi got a deal on a miscellany of small fish and a couple of heads, he would make a fish soup for which he was famous. The heads, he said, and the variety of fish and shellfish were what made the soup so hauntingly good. If he found hake, he would cook it in a small amount of water, aromatized by simmering some parsley, an odd carrot, a celery stalk, and perhaps a small potato in it. When the fish was done, he dressed it with vinegar, salt, and garlic chopped very fine, all beaten into dense olive oil from our hills. I would have preferred lemon with fish instead of vinegar, but he wouldn't hear of it, rightly insisting, "Why spend money on expensive lemons when we had fragrant red vinegar made from our own Sangiovese wine?" Victor still asks for this excellent condiment when I cook a *branzino* in the same manner.

My son, Giuliano, was born in New York and was probably one of the last children of his generation in this country to reach voting age having rarely had a meal that wasn't prepared at home, from scratch and with fresh ingredients, by a close relation—sometimes by his grandparents, mostly by his mother. He was fortunate in this and, it may be allowed, he was fortunate as well in the cooks that fate chose to look after him. From the beginning, no inhibitions impaired his enjoyment of everything that came to the table, and over time, he became an active participant in its production. Our family cooking provided the frame that he now fills with life every day.

Giuliano was eleven before my cooking took a professional turn. Until then, I had cooked by rifling through my taste memories of all the meals that my mother and my father and his mother had made. Every holiday spawned a different memory: Christmas brought cappelletti; New Year's, cotechino with lentils; Easter, milk-fed lamb, fava beans, and artichokes. All this you can find in my first cookbook, which, with its pastas and soups, its veal and fish dishes, its vegetables, and its homey desserts, is largely a record of what I ate before I was married. And now, in these pages, you are vouchsafed a look at my son's own account of the sources from which he nourishes himself and his family today.

The recipes Giuliano has chosen and brought up to date derive from the traditional cooking of our families. There is more to that tradition, however, than a mere sum of its recipes. It is the act of cooking itself that constitutes tradition, a tradition that looks to the production of a fresh meal for the family as the manifestation of a bond of affection and kinship, as the affirmation of identity, as a personal moment of nourishment and celebration.

MARCELLA HAZAN

In my late teens, with my mother in Florence, Italy.

Introduction

I was fortunate to eat very well while I was growing up. Many people reading this probably know that my mother is a very good cook, but I also had the privilege of enjoying the food of two other women with exceptional cooking skills: my grandmothers, Nonna Giulia and Nonna Mary.

Nonna Giulia and Nonno David were my paternal grandparents. They were Sephardic Jews who settled in Italy and fled to the United States when my father was eight years old, just before the Second World War. Nonna Giulia set a gracious table. The aromas emanating from her kitchen drew not only our family but also friends and neighbors. The kitchen was her domain, a place where men weren't allowed. Whether it was a simple preparation of the fish we caught from my grandparents' dock at Atlantic Beach or her *bamya*, a baked okra dish likely handed down to her by her mother, everything was made with care and love, and I remember eagerly looking forward to Friday night Shabbat dinners at her house. Presentation was important, so her elegant table was always covered with a beautiful tablecloth, but the food itself always took precedence.

Nonna Mary and Nonno Fin were my maternal grandparents; Nonna Mary's table was less formal, but her cooking was no less delicious than Nonna Giulia's. Her repertoire included Arab-influenced dishes learned during her time living in Egypt, as well as the wonderfully rich cuisine of the Emilia-Romagna region in Italy. Growing up, I was fortunate enough to spend every summer with her near the beach in Cesenatico. I remember sitting in her kitchen as she cooked. Of the many dishes she prepared, one of my favorites was her tortelloni filled with Swiss chard. Once, at age four, I ate so many that I collapsed at the table; when the doctor was called, he assured my terrified grandmother that I was just happily satiated and fast asleep.

When I was a child, it never occurred to me that one day I would have to cook for myself if I wanted to continue eating the food to which I was accustomed. The realization came on a middle-school trip; I could barely endure the food and, deciding to volunteer for kitchen duty, called my mother for recipes. In college, during what were probably my skinniest years, I participated in a program called "served meal," which was run entirely by students. A student maître d' took reservations and seated the guests (other students), student waiters took orders and served, and student cooks prepared the food. I, of course, offered to cook, with the understanding that I would partake of the food I prepared.

I like to tell people I learned to cook through osmosis. I remember often sitting in my mother's kitchen and occasionally getting to help. Unlike most cooks, my mother did not like to taste when she was cooking. She would use her sense of smell to monitor the flavors and, if I was around, always called on me to do the tasting and let her know if the dish needed anything. I became my mother's official taster; she would say my palate was the equivalent of perfect pitch (the latter being something I most definitely do not possess). When I finally left home, I had acquired taste memories that would guide me when I began cooking for myself. After I graduated from college, I spent a year living in Italy, in an apartment next door to my Nonna Mary in Cesenatico. During that time I often prepared meals for both of us. Already in her eighties, my nonna was slowing down a bit (though she lived to the ripe old age of 101), and she appreciated it when someone else would cook for her. She was always supportive of my kitchen forays and taught me some of her specialties, like the Savoy cabbage rolls filled with lamb and rice that I've included in this book. Nonna Mary had a sweet tooth, and I remember frequently having her *ciambella* for breakfast.

I usually cringe when I am asked to name my favorite dish; I like so many different foods that it is difficult to choose. I usually say that I don't have favorites, but that is not really true. Growing up, there were definitely some dishes I looked forward to more than others. There are foods Nonna Mary and Nonna Giulia used to make, and when I encounter those flavors now, they bring back sweet memories of both my grandmothers. This book is about those flavors and those memories. I realized that many of those dishes were no longer in our daily repertoire and I hadn't eaten them in a long time. As my daughters reach the age of understanding, I find myself wanting to impart a bit of my history to them, because I feel it is important that those wonderful flavors not be forgotten.

Some of these dishes I set about trying to re-create simply by trial and error. Inevitably, some will have morphed into something new, as my memories of them have begun to fade. In many cases, a fifty-six-year-old notebook that my mother lent me, in which she wrote recipes dictated by her mother when my parents married, aided my memory. The recipes in that notebook were a far cry from the precise instructions my mother has become known for in her cookbooks, so a bit of interpretation was necessary, but as I cooked them, I felt confident that they were accurate representations of what my grandmother used to make.

Unlike me, my mother had had little interest in watching her mother cook. But then she married my father, who, as my mother always likes to say, could put up with a lot of things, but not a bad meal. She suddenly found herself needing to cook and discovered that, with some guidance, a natural instinct emerged—as well as memories of the flavors she had grown up with, which had been buried in her subconscious. Luckily, that gene seems to have been passed on to me.

Of course, many of the favorite dishes of my childhood were ones my mother made that were not necessarily what my grandmother used to cook. Some of these recipes have appeared in my mother's cookbooks, but as I've been preparing them over the years, subtle changes have naturally occurred. In fact, my father maintains that he can tell whether my mother's beloved butter, onion, and tomato sauce—which only uses four ingredients, including the salt—has been made by her or by me.

I did not want to limit this book to the past, however, so I have included new family favorites as well—some found during our yearly expeditions in Italy, others inspired by adventures at the local market—each of which is now made often and much beloved. Our girls—Gabriella, now twelve, and Michela, now seven—often want to help me cook. Gabriella is already making meals from start to finish, and, with my help, Michela is starting to as well. They are both quite proficient at making homemade pasta, and Gabriella loves to bake—something I couldn't be happier about, because dessert has always been my least favorite part of the meal to create. I've also included dishes my wife likes to make, although sadly for me, she most often cooks when I'm traveling.

Not surprisingly, mealtimes are an important part of our family's day, and we always make every effort to sit down to dinner together. Sharing meals allows our family to reconnect and enjoy each other's company. The food served is just as important as the conversation—after all, good memories are created from satisfying sensations—and my goal in writing this book is to share the ways in which we sustain our family with flavor and joy.

Chapter 1:

Appetizers, Salads, and Side Dishes

The classic Italian meal consists of several courses, none of which is considered a main course. A *primo*, or first course, can be a pasta, risotto, or soup. It is followed by a *secondo*, a second course that usually consists of meat, chicken, or fish, often accompanied by a vegetable. The *secondo* is followed by a salad, and then by fruit or dessert. A simple green salad is a part of almost every one of our family meals, and we like to serve it at the end as a refreshing palate cleanser. Some salads, such as the Tuna, Bean, and Red Onion Salad in this chapter (see page 34), can also be a light meal or an appetizer. There's also a "Russian" salad here (see page 30), a typical holiday dish that has nothing to do with Russia except for the fact that it has beets in it; I remember my parents would almost always make it to celebrate the New Year.

When we are in the States, we miss the pizza from our favorite *pizzerie* in Italy, so we sometimes make a home-style baker's pizza that does not require a professional wood-burning pizza oven. Our kids love to participate in making it; I'll never forget a deep-blue pizza our daughter Gabriella once made by mixing food coloring into the dough. For one of our girls' birthdays, we threw a pizza party. I prepared the dough the day before, giving it time to rest. The day of the party, we put out a variety of toppings and everyone made their own pizza.

Pizza

Time from start to finish: 9 hours

SERVES 4

1. To make the starter, mix the lukewarm water, yeast, and sugar in a small bowl. Let it rest for 10 minutes.

2. Put the flour, cool water, salt, and olive oil in a stand mixer fitted with a dough hook or in a food processor. Add the starter, and mix at moderate speed or run the processor just until a homogeneous dough forms, usually less than 1 minute. Coat the inside of a mixing bowl with a little olive oil and place the dough in the bowl. Cover with plastic wrap and let the dough rise for at least 8 and up to 12 hours. Alternatively, after the dough has risen for 8 hours, you can refrigerate it for up to 24 hours. Remove it from the refrigerator at least 30 minutes before using it.

3. When you are ready to assemble the pizza, preheat the oven to the highest temperature possible, preferably the convection heat setting, if available; if not, use the regular bake setting.

4. Roll out the dough about ¼ inch thick, sprinkling flour on the counter and the rolling pin as needed to prevent the dough from sticking. If you are using a rectangular baking sheet to cook the pizza, roll the dough into an oval shape; if your baking sheet is square, roll it into a circle.

5. Lightly coat the baking sheet with olive oil. Transfer the dough to the baking sheet and stretch it with your fingers to fit. Add your desired topping and bake until the edges of the dough begin to brown, 10 to 15 minutes. Cut into pieces and serve hot.

¼ cup lukewarm water

1 package active dry yeast
(¼ ounce)

1 teaspoon sugar

4¼ cups all-purpose flour

1 cup plus 2 tablespoons cool (not ice) water

1 tablespoon plus 2 teaspoons salt

2 tablespoons extra-virgin olive oil

Topping of your choice
(pages 20–21)

Pizza Toppings

FOR CLASSIC MARGHERITA TOPPING

2 cups canned whole peeled tomatoes with their juice

2 tablespoons extra-virgin olive oil

Salt

1 pound buffalo-milk mozzarella (if unavailable, use regular whole-milk mozzarella)

1 teaspoon dried oregano leaves

FOR SAUSAGE TOPPING

All the ingredients for Classic Margherita Topping (above)

8 ounces cooked mild pork sausage

FOR PROSCIUTTO TOPPING

All the ingredients for Classic Margherita Topping (above)

4 ounces thinly sliced prosciutto

FOR GRILLED VEGETABLE TOPPING

All the ingredients for Classic Margherita Topping (above)

½ recipe Grilled Zucchini (page 53)

½ recipe Roasted Peppers (page 51)

CLASSIC MARGHERITA TOPPING

1. Coarsely chop the tomatoes. Put 1 tablespoon of the olive oil in a 10-inch skillet over medium-high heat. When the oil is hot, add the tomatoes with their juice and season with salt to taste. Cook until the tomatoes are no longer watery, 10 to 15 minutes.

2. While the tomatoes are cooking, cut the mozzarella into ¼-inch dice.

3. Spread the tomatoes over the dough and sprinkle with the mozzarella. Season lightly with salt and sprinkle with the oregano. Finish by drizzling the remaining tablespoon olive oil on top.

SAUSAGE TOPPING

1. Follow the instructions for the Margherita topping.

2. Crumble the cooked sausage evenly over the pizza.

PROSCIUTTO TOPPING

1. Follow the instructions for the Margherita topping.

2. Arrange the slices of prosciutto evenly over the pizza.

GRILLED VEGETABLE TOPPING

1. Follow the instructions for the Margherita topping.

2. Arrange the grilled vegetables evenly over the pizza.

SAUTÉED MUSHROOM TOPPING

1. Follow the instructions for the Margherita topping.

2. Peel and finely chop the garlic clove. Finely chop enough parsley leaves to measure about 1 tablespoon. With a paper towel, gently brush any dirt from the mushrooms and thinly slice them. Put the olive oil, garlic, and parsley in a 10-inch skillet over medium-high heat. When the garlic is sizzling, add the mushrooms and season with salt and pepper. Cook until the mushrooms are tender and all the liquid they release has evaporated, about 10 minutes.

3. Spread the sautéed mushrooms evenly over the pizza.

ANCHOVY TOPPING

1. Follow the instructions for the Margherita topping.

2. Arrange the anchovies evenly over the pizza.

ALLA MARINARA (CLASSIC NEAPOLITAN PIZZA TOPPING)

1. Follow the instructions for the Margherita topping, omitting the mozzarella and oregano.

2. Peel and thinly slice the garlic. Sprinkle the garlic over the pizza.

FOR SAUTÉED MUSHROOM TOPPING

All the ingredients for Classic Margherita Topping (page 20)

1 clove garlic

3 to 4 sprigs flat-leaf Italian parsley

8 ounces fresh white or cremini mushrooms

2 tablespoons extra-virgin olive oil

Salt

Freshly ground black pepper

FOR ANCHOVY TOPPING

All the ingredients for Classic Margherita Topping (page 20)

12 anchovy fillets

FOR ALLA MARINARA

All the ingredients for Classic Margherita Topping (page 20), except the mozzarella and oregano

3 cloves garlic

Borekitas

Time from start to finish: 1 hour and 15 minutes

FOR THE DOUGH

4 tablespoons butter

1½ cups all-purpose flour

¼ cup vegetable oil

¼ teaspoon salt

FOR THE SPINACH FILLING

½ teaspoon salt

8 ounces fresh spinach, washed

1 ounce feta cheese

2 tablespoons whole-milk ricotta cheese

FOR THE CHEESE FILLING

½ cup freshly grated Parmigiano-Reggiano

5 ounces feta cheese

⅔ cup whole-milk ricotta cheese

My parents and I went to my grandparents' almost every Friday for Shabbat dinner. I can still taste and smell the wonderful little pies my Nonna Giulia made, which she called *borekitas*. She made them either with a dough shell or a phyllo shell. The fillings were spinach or cheese. In attempting to replicate them, I used Claudia Roden's *The Book of Jewish Food* as a guide. Both the cheese and spinach fillings below are just like what I remember, and the dough shell, my favorite of the two, is just as good as the one Nonna Giulia used to make.

MAKES ABOUT 20 *BOREKITAS*

DOUGH

1. Cut the butter into small pieces and allow to come to room temperature.

2. Put all the ingredients in a food processor with ¼ cup water and run it until a smooth, homogeneous dough forms. If it crumbles when pinched, mix in a little more water, 1 tablespoon at a time, until the dough is soft and smooth when pinched.

3. Wrap the dough in plastic and let it rest for about 20 minutes before using.

SPINACH FILLING

1. In a pot large enough to cook the spinach, put about 2 inches of water, and place over high heat. When the water is boiling, add the salt and spinach. Cook until tender, 2 to 3 minutes, then drain.

2. Once the spinach is cool enough to handle, squeeze the excess water out and coarsely chop. Place the spinach in a bowl. Crumble the feta and add it along with the ricotta. Mix thoroughly.

CHEESE FILLING

1. Put all three cheeses in a bowl and mix thoroughly.

1. Preheat the oven to 350°F on the bake setting.

2. Take about a walnut-size ball of dough, place it on a counter, and press it with your fingers into a disk 2 inches in diameter. Put about 1 tablespoon of either cheese or spinach filling on the disk. Fold the disk over the filling to form a half-moon shape, making sure to pinch the open sides together to seal them, and place on a baking sheet, either oiled or lined with a nonstick baking mat.

3. When all the *borekitas* are assembled, bake until golden brown, about 20 minutes. Serve warm.

My daughters Gabriella (right) and Michela (left) kneading dough.

Frittata with Artichokes

Time from start to finish: 45 minutes

1 lemon

2 artichokes

½ medium yellow onion

2 tablespoons extra-virgin olive oil

3 to 4 sprigs flat-leaf Italian parsley

Salt

5 eggs

½ tablespoon butter

A frittata is basically an open-faced omelet in which the filling is mixed into the eggs rather than surrounded by them. I like *frittate* served both hot and cold. A cold frittata makes a terrific sandwich filling, and I remember my mother often made me a frittata sandwich to take to school for lunch. My favorite, the artichoke frittata, was unfortunately also the most labor-intensive because of having to trim the artichokes. Don't substitute preserved, canned, or frozen artichokes, though—the difference from fresh is like night and day, and once you get the hang of it, it will take you less than five minutes to trim an artichoke.

SERVES 4

1. Squeeze the juice of the lemon into a bowl of cold water. Trim all the tough parts from the artichokes: Snap the leaves back, leaving behind the tender parts at the bottom, and use a paring knife to trim off all the dark-green parts. Cut off the stems and trim the outer green rings, saving only the white centers; slice and put in the bowl of lemon water. Scoop out the chokes, scraping the hearts clean with a round-tipped dinner knife. Cut each artichoke heart in half lengthwise and then into thin slices. Place the slices in the bowl of lemon water.

2. Peel and finely chop the onion. Place it with the olive oil in a 10-inch nonstick ovenproof skillet over medium-high heat. Sauté until the onion turns a rich golden color, about 5 minutes.

3. While the onion is sautéing, finely chop enough parsley leaves to measure about 1 tablespoon. When the onion is ready, drain the artichokes and add them to the pan along with the parsley. Season with salt, stir well, then add ½ cup water. Cover the pan and cook until the artichokes are tender, 10 to 15 minutes. If there is still liquid in the pan when the artichokes are ready, raise the heat and cook, uncovered, to evaporate any remaining liquid.

4. While the artichokes are cooking, put the eggs in a mixing bowl and beat until the yolks and whites are evenly mixed. When the artichokes are ready, transfer them to the bowl with the eggs and mix thoroughly.

5. Preheat the broiler.

6. Put the butter in the skillet and return to medium heat. When the butter is hot, pour in the egg-and-artichoke mixture. Cook over medium heat for 6 minutes, then place under the broiler until the top is lightly browned, about 2 minutes. Slide the frittata onto a cutting board. Cut into slices and serve hot or at room temperature.

At six years old, in Northern
Italy with my mother.

Frittata with Pancetta and Potatoes

Time from start to finish: about 50 minutes

∽∾∽∾∽∾∽∾∽∾∽∾∽∾∽∾∽∾∽∾∽∾∽∾∽∾∽∾∽∾

½ pound red potatoes

½ large sweet yellow onion

2 ounces pancetta, sliced ½ inch thick

2 tablespoons butter

Salt

5 eggs

Freshly ground black pepper

Eggs and bacon with a side of potatoes seems like the all-American breakfast, but it also makes a delicious frittata that's as good cold as it is hot. I like the texture of red potatoes here, but not their skin, so I use larger potatoes, which are easier to peel.

∽∾∽∾∽∾∽∾∽∾∽∾∽∾∽∾∽∾∽∾∽∾∽∾∽∾∽∾∽∾

SERVES 4

1. Put the potatoes in a saucepan and cover with water. Place over high heat and cover the pan. When the water is boiling, reduce the heat to medium-low and cook the potatoes until tender, 25 to 30 minutes, depending on size. Remove the potatoes and peel them as soon as they are cool enough to handle.

2. While the potatoes are cooking, peel and thinly slice the onion crosswise. Unravel the pancetta and cut into narrow strips.

3. Put 1½ tablespoons of the butter in a 10-inch nonstick, ovenproof skillet over medium heat. When the butter has melted, add the pancetta and sauté until it has lost its raw color. Add the onion, season lightly with salt, and continue sautéing until the onion has softened and turned a light caramel color, 8 to 10 minutes.

4. While the onion is sautéing, cut the potatoes in half and slice the halves into half moons about ⅛ inch thick. Put the eggs in a mixing bowl and beat until the yolks and whites are evenly mixed.

5. When the onion is ready, add the potatoes, season with salt and pepper, and toss until the potatoes are evenly mixed with the onions and pancetta. Transfer the contents of the pan to the bowl with the eggs and mix thoroughly.

6. Preheat the broiler.

7. Put the remaining ¹/₂ tablespoon butter in the skillet and return to medium heat. When the butter is hot, pour in the egg-and-potato mixture. Cook over medium heat for 6 minutes, then place under the broiler until the top is lightly browned, about 2 minutes. Slide the frittata onto a cutting board. Cut into slices and serve hot or at room temperature.

My daughters tasting the chocolate mousse they helped me make.

Frittata with Zucchini

Time from start to finish: 35 minutes

½ large sweet yellow onion

3 tablespoons butter

Salt

12 ounces zucchini, preferably small ones

Freshly ground black pepper

5 eggs

One of the vegetable dishes my mother used to teach students at her school in Bologna is *Zucchine alla Brianzola*, zucchini sautéed with lots of caramelized onions. I used to love this dish best, and have discovered that it also makes a delicious frittata!

SERVES 4

1. Peel and thinly slice the onion crosswise. Put 2½ tablespoons of the butter in a 10-inch nonstick, ovenproof skillet over medium heat. When the butter has melted, add the onion and season lightly with salt. Sauté until the onion has softened and turned a light caramel color, 8 to 10 minutes.

2. While the onion is sautéing, wash the zucchini, remove the ends, and cut into thin rounds about ⅛ inch thick. When the onion is ready, add the zucchini and season with salt and pepper. Cook, stirring occasionally, until the zucchini is quite tender and has started to brown, 10 to 15 minutes.

3. While the zucchini is cooking, put the eggs in a mixing bowl and beat until the yolks and whites are evenly mixed.

4. When the zucchini is ready, transfer the contents of the pan to the bowl with the eggs and mix thoroughly.

5. Preheat the broiler.

6. Put the remaining ½ tablespoon butter in the skillet and return to medium heat. When the butter is hot, pour in the egg-and-zucchini mixture. Cook over medium heat for 6 minutes, then place under the broiler until the top is lightly browned, about 2 minutes. Slide the frittata onto a cutting board. Cut into slices and serve hot or at room temperature.

Homemade Mayonnaise

Time from start to finish: 15 minutes

This mayonnaise is used in Insalata Russa (page 30) and is wonderful with poached fish. Homemade mayonnaise is one of the first things my mother taught me how to make, perhaps because it doesn't involve using the stove. It's not difficult to make but you do have to be careful to avoid "breaking" the mayonnaise, which is when the solids separate and you end up with a grainy, liquid mess—something I remember doing a few times when I was learning. The trickiest part is when you begin adding oil. At first you need to add it slowly, just a little at a time. You don't want to overwhip the eggs either, so as soon as you see that the oil has been incorporated into the mayonnaise, more needs to be added. Some people may be concerned about eating a raw-egg product. The odds are definitely against getting sick, but to be perfectly safe, you can use pasteurized shell eggs. They can be used just like regular eggs, and there is no difference in how the mayonnaise turns out.

2 egg yolks, at room temperature

½ teaspoon salt, or more to taste

1½ cups vegetable oil

2 tablespoons freshly squeezed lemon juice, or more to taste

MAKES ABOUT 1¼ CUPS

1. Put the egg yolks in the bowl of an electric mixer fitted with a whisk attachment.

2. Add the salt and begin beating on medium-high. Beat until the yolks become creamy in consistency and pale in color, 2 to 3 minutes. Begin adding the oil, very slowly at first, pausing periodically to allow it to be incorporated into the eggs. After about ¼ cup of the oil has been added, begin adding the lemon juice, ½ tablespoon at a time. Don't be concerned if the consistency becomes looser. As more oil is beaten in, the mayonnaise will firm up again and then more lemon can be added, ½ tablespoon at a time. Continue until all the oil and lemon juice have been incorporated. Taste, and add more salt or lemon juice if desired. This mayonnaise can be stored in the refrigerator for 2 to 3 days.

Insalata Russa

Time from start to finish: 3 hours and 30 minutes

As far as I know, the only reason this salad is called "Russian" is because of the red color from the beets in it. Although you can make this in about half the time by using canned beets, fresh, baked beets are far superior and can easily be prepared the day before. This is often one of the salads on display at the best gourmet shops in Italy, such as Peck in Milan and Tamburini in Bologna. It is a very festive dish that my mother usually made for New Year's Eve. Though somewhat labor-intensive, it is definitely worth the effort for any special occasion. It's also one of the few Italian dishes whose appearance is as important as its flavor. Decorating it was a family affair, with each of us contributing. I remember I used to make flowers using a green bean for the stem and beets cut into ovals for the petals surrounding a carrot disk. You can let your imagination run free, using the vegetables as your palette.

SERVES 6

1. If using fresh beets, preheat the oven to 400°F. Wash the beets under cold water and cut the tops away from the root bulbs. Put the wet bulbs on a sheet of heavy-duty aluminum foil and seal them in a pouch, allowing enough space inside for steam to circulate. Place the pouches on a baking sheet and bake until the beets are tender when pierced with a toothpick, about 1½ hours.

2. Fill three 4-quart pots with water. Put the potatoes in one pot and place all three pots over high heat. Peel the carrots and set them aside.

3. Once the pot with the potatoes comes to a boil, lower the heat to medium-low and cook until the potatoes are tender, 25 to 30 minutes. Remove the potatoes and peel them as soon as they are cool enough to handle.

4. When one of the other two pots comes to a boil, add 2 teaspoons salt, 1 tablespoon of the red wine vinegar, and the shrimp. Cover and cook until the shrimp have turned pink, usually by the time the water has returned to a boil. Drain, and when the shrimp are cool enough to handle, remove the shells and devein, if necessary. Put half of the shrimp aside and cut the rest into pieces no larger than ½ inch.

5. When the remaining pot comes to a boil, add 2 teaspoons salt and the carrots. Cook until the carrots are tender, 10 to 12 minutes, then remove the carrots and set aside.

---

2 fresh beets, or 6 canned small whole beets, drained

½ pound red potatoes

2 medium carrots

Salt

2 tablespoons red wine vinegar

1 pound large shrimp (21 to 25 per pound)

4 ounces green beans

4 ounces frozen peas

4 cornichons (pickled gherkins)

2 tablespoons capers

3 tablespoons extra-virgin olive oil

1 recipe Homemade Mayonnaise (page 29)

6. While the carrots are cooking, trim both ends off all the green beans. After removing the carrots from the pot, add the green beans to the same pot. Cook until tender, about 8 minutes. Scoop the beans out and add the frozen peas. Cook for 3 minutes, then drain.

7. While the beans and peas are cooking, cut the potatoes into ¼-inch dice. Cut the carrots into ¼-inch dice, but save a few round disks for decoration. Peel the beets (if using fresh) and cut into ¼-inch dice, but save about one-quarter of a beet for decoration. Finely dice the cornichons. When the green beans are done, cut them into ¼-inch dice.

8. Put the shrimp pieces, the cornichons, the capers, and all the vegetables in a large mixing bowl. Add the olive oil and the remaining vinegar and season lightly with salt. Toss until everything is evenly coated with the olive oil. Add half of the mayonnaise and mix it in well. Pour the mixture onto a flat serving platter and shape it into a flat-topped oval or circle. Use the remaining mayonnaise to cover the entire surface.

9. Decorate by placing the whole shrimp around the edges and using the reserved vegetables, as suggested in the head note above.

Making a toast with my parents in our kitchen.

Insalata Mista

Time from start to finish: 15 minutes

We usually serve a salad at the end of the meal in Italy. It is refreshing and cleanses the palate. At home we have a salad like this almost every day and our girls have learned how to dress it. I taught them the same way I learned it from my parents, using a proverb rather than a recipe. The proverb says you need four people: a wise person for the salt, a generous person for the extra-virgin olive oil, a stingy person for the red wine vinegar, and a patient person to toss—thirty-four times, according to my father—so that every bite is evenly coated. I sometimes add a fifth person: a wealthy person for good balsamic vinegar. Not the twenty-five-year-old *aceto balsamico tradizionale*, but a younger, six- or seven-year-old balsamic often referred to by top balsamic vinegar producers as *condimento balsamico*. Occasionally we vary the ingredients, adding radicchio, Belgian endive, arugula, cucumber, grated carrots, or sliced avocado, or a combination.

1 large or 2 small heads lettuce (green- or red-leaf, oak-leaf, Boston, or romaine)

1 red or yellow bell pepper (or ½ of each)

½ fennel bulb

1 ripe tomato

Salt

4 tablespoons extra-virgin olive oil

1½ tablespoons red wine vinegar

SERVES 4 TO 6

1. Tear the lettuce leaves into bite-size pieces and transfer to a salad bowl.

2. Wash the bell pepper and cut it into narrow strips about 1¹/₂ inches long. Wash the fennel and thinly slice it crosswise. Wash the tomato, remove the core, and cut it into wedges. Add the bell pepper, fennel, and tomato to the salad bowl.

3. Season with salt and add the olive oil and vinegar. Toss well and serve at once.

Tuna, Bean, and Red Onion Salad

Time from start to finish: 20 minutes

½ small red onion or other sweet onion

7 ounces canned tuna packed in olive oil, drained

2 cups canned cannellini beans, drained

Salt

Freshly ground black pepper

3 tablespoons extra-virgin olive oil

1 tablespoon red wine vinegar

This is a great salad for a light lunch. It's also perfect to bring on a picnic. If the idea of canned tuna does not appeal to you, understand that I never intended this to be made with the bland tuna packed in water that is commonly available in the supermarket. In Italy, canned tuna is a delicacy. Packed in big chunks in extra-virgin olive oil, it is so succulent and flavorful you could eat it straight from the can—or jar, as the best is usually packaged in glass. The ultimate is called *ventresca*, and it comes from the fattier belly of the tuna. If you are familiar with Japanese sushi, it is the equivalent of *toro*.

I soak the onion in cold water to take some of the sharpness away. If you are going to make the salad ahead of time, keep the onion separate until you are ready to serve; otherwise it may permeate the salad. If I am going on a picnic, I'll keep the onion in a zip-top bag and toss it in at the last minute.

SERVES 4

1. Peel the onion and thinly slice it crosswise. Put it in a bowl and cover with cold water. Soak for 15 minutes.

2. Place the tuna in a serving bowl and, using a fork, break the chunks into large flakes. Add the beans. Drain the red onion and add it to the bowl. Season with salt and pepper, add the olive oil and vinegar, and toss thoroughly. Serve at room temperature.

Roman-Style Chicory Salad

Time from start to finish: 25 minutes

4 medium cloves garlic

2 tablespoons red wine vinegar

3 anchovy fillets

1 pound Belgian endive or chicory

Salt

4 tablespoons extra-virgin olive oil

Freshly ground black pepper

One of the times I visited my parents while they were living in Venice, my mother prepared this wonderfully fresh, just slightly bitter salad with a robust, garlic-scented anchovy dressing. It was my introduction to *puntarelle*, Roman argot for a variety of chicory that is in season in the winter. Actually the word means "tips" and refers to the white shoots in the center, which are the parts used in this salad. When my parents had me over to their condo on Longboat Key to celebrate a recent birthday, they surprised me with a *puntarelle* salad. My father, who has discovered online shopping, had had the vegetable shipped from the West Coast. Although occasionally available in certain parts of the country, it is still pretty hard to find. It reminded me how much I like that salad, and I decided to adapt it to more readily available chicory and Belgian endive.

SERVES 4

1. Peel the garlic cloves and lightly crush them with either a meat pounder or a knife handle. Place them in a small bowl with the vinegar. Finely chop the anchovies and add them to the bowl. Mix well and let stand for at least 20 minutes or up to 1 hour.

2. When you are ready to serve the salad, wash the endive or chicory and dry it in a salad spinner or with a dry towel. Transfer to a salad bowl. Discard the garlic cloves and pour the vinegar-and-anchovy mixture over the salad. Season lightly with salt; add the olive oil and several grindings from the pepper mill. Serve immediately.

Asparagus Fritters

Time from start to finish: 30 minutes

Most people consider the asparagus tip to be the best part, yet both our girls at first would only eat the bottoms. The fact is that the bottom is the sweetest part, but for it to be edible, the tough outer layer must be removed. After cutting off the woody bottom of the asparagus spear, I always peel the remaining bottom third, removing any tough skin and leaving only the tender, sweet flesh. I'm also a firm believer in fat asparagus as opposed to thin. I find it sweeter and, frankly, much easier to peel, not to mention that there will be fewer to peel. Even kids who usually have misgivings about vegetables will like these fritters. Lightly crisp on the outside and tender on the inside, they are irresistible.

1 pound asparagus

Salt

1 egg

⅓ cup whole milk

⅓ cup all-purpose flour

Vegetable oil

MAKES ABOUT 15 FRITTERS

1. Fill a 12-inch skillet with water and place over high heat. Cut off the white, woody bottom part of each asparagus spear, then peel the remaining bottom third. Add 1 teaspoon salt to the boiling water, then gently slide in the asparagus. Cook for 5 to 6 minutes, or until the asparagus spears are tender, then lift them out and set aside.

2. Break the egg into a medium mixing bowl and add the milk. Beat with a whisk until the egg and milk are evenly mixed together. Add the flour and continue whisking until smooth.

3. Put the cooked asparagus in a food processor and pulse until creamy. Add the asparagus to the mixing bowl, season with about ½ teaspoon salt, and mix well with a spoon.

4. Cover a plate with a paper towel. Put enough vegetable oil in an 8-inch skillet to come ¼ inch up the sides of the pan and place over medium-high heat. Allow the oil to get very hot. Test to see if it is hot enough by placing a drop of the asparagus mixture in. It should sizzle and float to the surface.

5. When the oil is ready, fill a ¼-cup measure halfway with the asparagus mixture and pour it into the skillet. Repeat until the skillet is full without being crowded. When the bottom of a fritter is golden brown, usually after less than 1 minute, turn it with a slotted spatula. When the other side is also golden brown, lift the fritter, letting the excess oil drip back into the pan, and place it on the plate with the paper towel. Continue until you have used up all the asparagus mixture. Sprinkle the fritters with a little salt and serve. Careful, though, they're hot!

Baked Tomatoes

Time from start to finish: 1 hour

This is a gem from my mother's notebook of Nonna Mary's recipes. I remember Nonna Mary serving these tomatoes along with assorted grilled meats during the summer in Cesenatico. They are also a perfect accompaniment to veal cutlets, and together they make a great sandwich, one of my favorite lunches that my mother would pack for me to take to school.

½ loaf Italian bread (about 8 ounces)

5 to 6 sprigs flat-leaf Italian parsley

1 medium clove garlic

1 tablespoon capers

1 teaspoon salt

3 tablespoons extra-virgin olive oil, or more as needed

2 large tomatoes or 4 small ones

SERVES 4

1. Preheat the oven to 250°F. Cut away and discard the crust from the loaf of bread and cut the loaf in half lengthwise. Bake for 5 minutes on each side. Let cool for 10 to 15 minutes.

2. Raise the oven temperature to 350°F on convection heat or to 375°F in an oven without convection heat.

3. Cut the bread into chunks small enough to fit easily in a food processor. Place them in the food processor and pulse until you have fairly even crumbs that are not too fine. Set aside 1 cup of crumbs and reserve any extra for another use.

4. Finely chop enough parsley leaves to measure about 2 tablespoons. Peel and finely chop the garlic. Put the parsley, garlic, bread crumbs, capers, salt, and olive oil in a mixing bowl. Mix well until the ingredients are evenly distributed and the bread crumbs are well coated with the olive oil. If there doesn't seem to be enough olive oil to coat them all, add a little more.

5. Cut the tomatoes in half crosswise and scoop out all the seeds. Place the tomatoes, cut side up, on a baking sheet. Fill the cavities with a generous amount of the bread-crumb mixture, heaping it on top of each tomato half.

6. Bake until a brown crust forms, about 20 minutes. Serve hot or at room temperature.

Braised Leeks and Peas

Time from start to finish: 45 minutes

5 to 6 sprigs flat-leaf Italian parsley

1 medium clove garlic

3 to 4 leeks

4 tablespoons extra-virgin olive oil

Salt

1¾ pounds fresh peas in the pod (or 12 ounces frozen)

Freshly ground black pepper

The first time I made this dish, I didn't check the pan often enough, and the vegetables almost burned when all the liquid evaporated. It came out very tasty, however, and our daughter Gabriella loved it. She named it "burned leeks and peas" and declared it one of her favorite vegetable dishes. I try to re-create that "almost burned" effect whenever I make the dish now, though Gabriella's assessment is often "not quite burned enough."

SERVES 4

1. Finely chop enough parsley leaves to measure about 2 tablespoons. Peel and finely chop the garlic.

2. Trim the tough green tops of the leeks. Cut off the roots and slice each leek in half crosswise and in quarters lengthwise. Place in a bowl with cold water and swish them around to loosen any dirt.

3. Put the olive oil, garlic, and parsley in a deep skillet over medium-high heat. Once the garlic is sizzling, lift the leeks out of the water and add them to the pan. Season with salt and stir to coat the leeks well. Add enough water to come ½ inch up the sides of the pan, cover the pan, and cook the leeks for about 10 minutes if using fresh peas, and 20 minutes, if you're using frozen ones.

4. While the leeks are cooking, shell the peas, if using fresh. When the leeks are ready, add the peas, season with a little more salt and some grindings of black pepper, and add some more water to bring the level back to ½ inch up the sides of the pan. Cook, covered, until the peas are tender. This will take another 15 to 20 minutes for fresh peas and about 8 minutes for frozen.

5. Uncover the pan, raise the heat to high, and let any liquid evaporate completely, lightly browning the vegetables. Serve with some good crunchy bread.

Okra with Fresh Tomatoes

Time from start to finish: 1 hour

Until I moved to the South and discovered fried okra, my only experience with this vegetable was at my grandmother Nonna Giulia's, where we would go for dinner every Friday for a Shabbat meal. I remember hoping to get some of the smaller *bamya*, as she called it, from the top layer where the browned, yummiest ones were. In fact, my grandfather would usually complain that they were not browned enough. Now that I live in Florida and see okra often at the market, I decided to try to re-create the dish. I believe my grandmother cooked it entirely in the oven, but I found that braising it first over the burner makes it sweeter and richer. Eating it now brings back memories of those wonderful meals with my grandparents, and the tenderness and love with which Nonna Giulia served them.

1 pound okra

1 medium clove garlic

½ small yellow onion

2 tablespoons extra-virgin olive oil

Salt

12 ounces fresh tomatoes

2 tablespoons freshly squeezed lemon juice

SERVES 4

1. Rinse the okra in cold water and cut off the stem ends. Peel and thinly slice the garlic.

2. Peel and finely chop the onion and place it with the olive oil in a 10-inch ovenproof skillet or shallow braising pan over medium-high heat. Sauté until the onion turns a rich golden color, about 5 minutes, then add the garlic. When the garlic begins to sizzle, add the okra and season with salt. Stir for about 30 seconds, then add ½ cup water. Adjust the heat to a steady simmer, cover, and cook until tender, about 20 minutes. Check the pan periodically and stir. If all the liquid evaporates before the okra is tender, add more water, ¼ cup at a time.

3. While the okra is cooking, preheat the oven to 400°F on convection heat, or 425°F in an oven without convection heat. Peel the tomatoes with a vegetable peeler and remove the seeds. Cut the tomato into ¾-inch dice.

4. When the okra is tender, remove from the heat (if there is still liquid in the pan, raise the heat and let it evaporate first). Top with the tomato pieces and season lightly with salt. Add the lemon juice and bake, uncovered, for 15 minutes, then change the oven setting to broil. Cook until the top begins to brown, about 5 minutes, then remove from the oven. Serve hot.

Brussels Sprouts Braised with Pancetta

Time from start to finish: 30 minutes

1 pound Brussels sprouts

Salt

½ large yellow onion

2 tablespoons butter

1 ounce pancetta, sliced ¼ inch thick

Freshly ground black pepper

Brussels sprouts probably rank up there with spinach on children's lists of least-liked vegetables. But the first time I made these for our family, my daughters couldn't get enough of them. The trick is to boil them first, which makes them lose their bitterness. These Brussels sprouts come out sweet and luscious, wonderfully juxtaposed with savory bits of pancetta.

SERVES 4

1. Fill a pot large enough to hold all the Brussels sprouts with water and place over high heat.

2. Remove any bruised outer leaves from the sprouts and use a paring knife to trim the root ends. When the water comes to a boil, add 1 teaspoon salt and the Brussels sprouts. Cook for 10 minutes, then drain.

3. While the sprouts are cooking, peel and finely chop the onion. Put the onion and the butter in a 12-inch skillet and place over medium-high heat. Stir the onion as it sautés until it turns a rich golden color, about 5 minutes.

4. Unravel the pancetta and cut it into thin strips. When the onion is ready, add the pancetta and sauté, stirring, until the pancetta loses its raw color, about 1 minute. Add the Brussels sprouts and season with salt and pepper. Add $^1/_2$ cup water, cover the pan, and cook for 10 minutes, stirring occasionally. Uncover the pan and continue cooking until all the liquid has evaporated and the Brussels sprouts just begin to brown. Serve hot.

+ **NOTE:** You can make these several hours ahead of time. When ready to serve, return the pan to a low heat until the Brussels sprouts are warm.

Fried Zucchini Blossoms

Time from start to finish: 25 minutes

1 dozen zucchini or squash blossoms

1 cup water, or more if needed

⅔ cup flour, or more if needed

Vegetable oil

Salt

One of the places we take our students during the week-long course we offer at our cooking school in Italy is the extraordinary food market in Padova. In the late spring and early summer, beautiful squash blossoms are usually available. If our daughters are with us, they will pull out their most irresistible puppy-dog looks, making it all but impossible for me not to buy them. The way we like them best is fried in a simple flour-and-water batter. In the end, I'm always glad I gave in.

SERVES 4

1. Remove the stamens from the blossoms and make sure the petals are open.

2. Put the water in a medium bowl and gradually add the flour while whisking to keep the mixture smooth. When all the flour has been mixed with water, the batter should have the consistency of buttermilk. If not, adjust by adding more flour or water.

3. Pour enough oil into an 8-inch skillet to come ³/₄ inch up the sides and place over high heat. The oil is hot enough when a drop of the batter sizzles and floats to the surface. Dip a blossom into the batter to coat it well, then lift it out, letting any excess batter drip back into the bowl. Gently place the blossom in the hot oil. Repeat with as many blossoms as will fit loosely in the skillet. When a light brown crust forms on the bottoms of the blossoms, turn them over. When the other side is also light brown, use a slotted spoon to lift them out of the pan, gently shaking any excess oil back into the skillet, and transfer them to a cooling rack or a platter lined with paper towels. Repeat the process with the remaining blossoms. It's best to replace each blossom in the pan as it is removed, rather than waiting until the pan is empty before frying the next batch, as this will maintain a more constant oil temperature.

4. When all the blossoms are done, sprinkle with salt and serve hot.

Nonno Fin's Beans

Time from start to finish: 30 minutes

When I was just a toddler, I destroyed one of my parents' cookbooks, Ada Boni's *Il Talismano della Felicità*, so that it was barely held together by its binding. Its cover, which is permanently etched in my memory, was of a rugged-looking man hungrily eating a bowl of beans. Somehow there is something very manly about a dish of beans. My father loves beans, I love beans, and so did my maternal grandfather, Nonno Fin, whose recipe this is. I wonder if it was that "bean gene" that made me attack that book.

2 medium cloves garlic

5 to 6 sprigs flat-leaf Italian parsley

3 tablespoons extra-virgin olive oil

¾ cup canned whole peeled tomatoes with their juice

3 cups canned cannellini beans, drained

Salt

Freshly ground black pepper

SERVES 4

1. Peel and finely chop the garlic. Finely chop enough parsley leaves to measure about 2 tablespoons. Put the garlic, parsley, and olive oil in a 2-quart saucepan over medium-high heat.

2. When all the garlic is sizzling, add the canned tomatoes and break them into small pieces with a wooden spoon. Cook for about 1 minute, then add the beans and season with salt and generous grindings of the pepper mill. Once the contents of the pan are bubbling, lower the heat to medium-low, cover the pan, and cook for 20 minutes, stirring occasionally. Serve hot or warm.

At three years old, on Nonno Fin's shoulders in Italy.

Green Beans Stewed with Tomatoes

Time from start to finish: 1 hour

½ large yellow onion

3 tablespoons extra-virgin olive oil

Salt

1 medium clove garlic

1 pound fresh tomatoes

1½ pounds green beans

Freshly ground black pepper

This is another of my favorite dishes my grandmother Giulia used to make. Because they cook only in the moisture the tomatoes release, these beans have a rich tomato flavor. Do not be alarmed by the length of time the beans cook in this recipe. Although they are usually tender in 8 minutes when cooked in boiling water, it takes much longer when they are stewed in tomatoes. I do like my green beans tender—not mushy, but tender enough for them to have a rich, sweet flavor. Crisp, halfway-cooked beans always seem to taste like grass.

SERVES 4

1. Peel and thinly slice the onion crosswise. Put it with the olive oil in a deep skillet or braising pan over medium-high heat. Season lightly with salt and sauté until the onion turns a rich golden color, 8 to 10 minutes.

2. While the onion is sautéing, peel and thinly slice the garlic. Peel and coarsely chop the tomatoes. Wash the green beans and trim both ends.

3. When the onion is ready, add the garlic, stir for about 30 seconds, then add the tomatoes and the green beans. Season with salt and pepper to taste and cook, covered, over medium heat until the beans are tender, about 40 minutes. Check the beans periodically, and if all the liquid evaporates before they are tender, add a little water. Serve hot or at room temperature.

Spinach and Chickpeas

Time from start to finish: 20 minutes

This is one of the dishes my grandmother Giulia often made on Friday nights and that my mother included in her book *Marcella's Italian Kitchen*. I made it often when I was first living on my own because it is so quick, easy, and wonderfully satisfying. Even now, when I make it, the first bite immediately takes me back to the dining table in my grandparents' apartment in New York. My recipe is almost exactly like my mother's, except that I like to use less olive oil and I've increased the proportion of chickpeas to spinach. My mother calls for peeling the chickpeas one by one, which I now never do, perhaps because it was usually my job when I was little!

The amount of spinach listed assumes short, thin stems, as are usually found in bags of prewashed spinach. If you are using farmer's-market spinach with thicker stems, remove them and adjust the quantity accordingly.

18 ounces washed fresh spinach leaves

Salt

1 (19-ounce) can chickpeas

4 tablespoons extra-virgin olive oil

4 tablespoons lemon juice

SERVES 4

1. Put the spinach, 1 teaspoon salt, and about 1 inch of water in a pot over medium-high heat. After the spinach has wilted completely, about 2 minutes, remove from the heat and drain well. Squeeze as much liquid out of the leaves as possible, by using tongs or by pressing them against the side of the colander with the back of a spoon.

2. Drain the chickpeas and put them in a saucepan with the spinach, olive oil, and lemon juice. Place over medium heat and cook, covered, for 10 minutes after the mixture begins to bubble. Taste and adjust for salt, and serve hot.

Italian Latkes

Time from start to finish: 50 minutes

6 ounces sweet yellow onion (about ½ medium onion)

12 ounces Yukon Gold potatoes

Salt

3 to 4 sprigs flat-leaf Italian parsley

Vegetable oil

3 tablespoons all-purpose flour

2 eggs

Freshly ground black pepper

As some may know, my mother had little interest in cooking before she married my father. Several of the recipes in this book come from a little fifty-six-year-old notebook in which my mother took notes of recipes her mother taught her to make. One of them literally made my jaw drop. It described something that has become a tradition in our home around Hanukkah. Every year, my wife, Lael, pulls out our friend Joan Nathan's book and we make latkes. She makes the mixture and I fry them. I couldn't believe it when, leafing through my mother's notebook, I came across the following description: "One to three potatoes and one onion grated raw." I discovered that a dish that I thought was a recent family tradition is also one that my grandmother used to make before I was born!

SERVES 4

1. Peel the onion and finely chop it. Peel the potatoes and grate them, using the large holes of a grater or a food processor disk. Put the onion and potatoes in a colander over a bowl or in a sink. Add ½ teaspoon salt, mix well, and let stand for 20 minutes.

2. Finely chop enough parsley leaves to measure about 1 tablespoon.

3. Put enough oil in a skillet to come ½ inch up the sides and place over medium-high heat. Squeeze excess liquid out of the onions and potatoes and place them in a mixing bowl with the parsley, flour, and eggs. Season with a few grindings from the pepper mill and mix well.

4. As soon as the oil is hot enough to make a bit of potato sizzle, use your hands to form patties that are about 2 inches wide and ½ inch thick, and carefully slide as many as will comfortably fit into the hot oil. Once the bottoms are lightly browned, turn the patties over to brown the other side. It should take about 1 minute on each side. Transfer the fried patties to a platter lined with paper towels. When all the mixture is used up, sprinkle with salt and serve hot.

Potato Fritters

Time from start to finish: about 1 hour

This is another of the gems from my mother's fifty-six-year-old notebook of my grandmother's recipes. It may sound similar to the previous recipe I've named "Italian Latkes," but it is actually quite different. These delectable fritters are made with fully cooked mashed potatoes, so they are crispy on the outside and creamy on the inside. To create that wonderful contrast in textures, you must fry them until they are well browned.

1 pound Yukon Gold potatoes

⅓ cup freshly grated Parmigiano-Reggiano

⅛ teaspoon freshly grated nutmeg

2 tablespoons all-purpose flour

1 egg

Vegetable oil

Salt

SERVES 4

1. Put the potatoes in a pot with a little more than enough water to cover them, cover the pot, and place over high heat. When the water comes to a boil, lower the heat to medium and cook until the potatoes are tender, about 30 minutes.

2. When the potatoes are ready, transfer them to a plate, and as soon as they are cool enough to handle, remove the skins. Place a food mill equipped with the disk with the largest holes over a mixing bowl, and mash the potatoes through it into the bowl. Add the grated cheese, nutmeg, flour, and egg, and mix thoroughly.

3. Pour enough vegetable oil in a skillet to come ½ inch up the sides and place over medium-high heat. When the oil is hot enough to make a bit of the potato mixture sizzle, use your hands to form patties of the potato mixture that are about 3 inches in diameter and 1 inch thick. Slide in as many as will comfortably fit in the skillet. Brown them well on one side, then turn them over and brown the other side. Transfer to a platter lined with paper towels. The fritters need to be well browned to be crispy, so be patient. It will take at least 2 minutes on each side to brown them properly.

4. When all the potato mixture is used up, sprinkle the fritters with salt and serve at once. They will not be good once they are cold.

A Series of Recipes for the Grill

Family vacations with my parents always involved food in some way. A memorable trip we took was one summer when I was in my early teens. My parents rented a station wagon and we drove from New York to Maine. The coast of Maine is quite dramatic, and having recently taken up photography as a new hobby, I took countless pictures of the waves breaking against the rocky coast with my new camera. It was lobster, however, that left me with the most indelible memory of our trip. We ate lobster practically every day. We usually ate dinner at a restaurant, but during the day, we used the hibachi grill we had brought with us to grill seafood, vegetables, and even fruit. One day, we had acquired live lobsters from the dock and decided we would grill them for lunch. As soon as the grill was hot, my parents put the lobsters on it . . . and they promptly walked off the grill. Although we are hardly a vegetarian family, we had no desire to inflict a slow, painful death on those poor creatures. On the other hand, they had been just caught and we were not going to forgo eating them. Fortunately, at the picnic table next to us was a family who obviously had more experience with grilling lobsters, and they showed us how to kill them quickly by plunging a knife right behind their eyes. We did finally enjoy our lobsters that day, but for the rest of the trip we ate lobster only at restaurants. I confess I have not grilled lobster since then. My favorite way to have it is boiled in water "as salty as the ocean" and dipped in melted butter and lemon.

We do still grill vegetables, however, and one of my daughters' favorites is grilled eggplant. Fruit is also delicious grilled, as its flavor and sweetness become more intense. The following recipes can be combined to create a feast for a large group. The onions, peppers, and zucchini can be mixed together to form a delicious grilled vegetable salad. Serve the eggplant, the mushrooms, and the fruit separately. All the vegetables can be served either warm or at room temperature. The fruit, however, is best served warm, so plan on grilling it last.

Grilled Onions

Time from start to finish: 25 minutes

SERVES 4

1. Heat a charcoal or gas grill.

2. Cut the onion in half crosswise and remove the outer skin. Use a paring knife to score the cut side of the onion in a crisscross pattern. Place the onion halves on the grill with the cut side down. When the side facing the fire has charred, turn the onion over carefully. Drizzle the cut side with some olive oil, letting it seep in between the cuts, and season with salt. Continue cooking the onion until it feels tender when prodded with a fork, 15 to 20 minutes. Remove it from the grill, cut each half into 4 parts, and place on a serving platter. Season with a drizzle of olive oil and a few grindings from the pepper mill.

1 large sweet yellow onion

About 2 tablespoons extra-virgin olive oil

Salt

Freshly ground black pepper

Roasted Peppers

Time from start to finish: 40 minutes

SERVES 4

1. Heat a charcoal or gas grill.

2. When the grill is hot, put the peppers on the grill. Turn them as they become charred, and remove them once they are blackened on all sides. Place them in a plastic bag and tie it shut. After about 15 minutes, remove the peppers from the plastic bag. Remove the skin, which should come off easily now. Cut the peppers open to remove the core and the seeds. Cut the peppers into pieces about 1 inch wide and place them on a serving platter. Drizzle the olive oil over them and season with salt.

2 red or yellow bell peppers (or 1 of each)

1 tablespoon extra-virgin olive oil

Salt

Grilled Belgian Endive
and Radicchio

Time from start to finish: 25 minutes

3 heads Belgian endive

2 heads red radicchio

Salt

About 3 tablespoons extra-virgin
olive oil

Freshly ground black pepper

SERVES 4

1. Heat a charcoal or gas grill.

2. Cut the Belgian endive in half lengthwise, make a cut at the root end, and place on
the grill with the cut side facing the fire. Do the same with the radicchio, except that
it should be cut in quarters. Turn the endive and radicchio over when they are lightly
charred. Season with salt and drizzle generously with olive oil. Continue cooking until
the leaves are tender, 15 to 20 minutes, then transfer to a serving platter. Season with
a drizzle of olive oil and a few grindings from the pepper mill.

Grilled Portobello Mushrooms

Time from start to finish: 20 minutes

1 small clove garlic

3 to 4 sprigs flat-leaf Italian parsley

4 portobello mushrooms

2 tablespoons extra-virgin olive oil

Salt

Freshly ground black pepper

SERVES 4

1. Heat a charcoal or gas grill.

2. Peel and finely chop the garlic. Finely chop enough parsley leaves to measure about 1
tablespoon. Separate the stems from the caps of the mushrooms, cut the stems in half
lengthwise, and place both caps and stems in a mixing bowl. Add the garlic, parsley,
and olive oil, and season with salt and pepper. Toss the mushrooms until they are well
coated, then place them on the grill. Cook until tender and lightly charred on both sides,
about 5 minutes on each side, then transfer to a serving platter.

Grilled Zucchini

Time from start to finish: 15 minutes

SERVES 4

1. Heat a charcoal or gas grill.

2. Remove the ends of the zucchini and cut lengthwise into ¼-inch-thick slices. Brush with some olive oil and season with salt. Place on the grill and cook until tender and lightly charred on both sides, 3 to 5 minutes on each side, then transfer to a serving platter and drizzle a little more olive oil over them.

3 small to medium zucchini

2 tablespoons extra-virgin olive oil

Salt

Grilled Eggplant

Time from start to finish: 30 minutes

SERVES 4

1. Heat a charcoal or gas grill.

2. Peel and finely chop the garlic. Finely chop enough parsley leaves to measure about 1 tablespoon. Put the parsley and garlic in a small bowl. Add the salt and 2 tablespoons of the olive oil and mix well with a spoon.

3. Cut off the tops of the eggplants and cut them in half lengthwise. Score the cut side with 6 diagonal cuts about ½ inch deep (do not cut all the way down to the skin). Brush the cut side with the remaining olive oil.

4. Put the eggplant, cut side down, on the hot grill and cook until they have grill marks, 2 to 3 minutes. Turn the eggplant over and spread the garlic-and-parsley mixture over each eggplant half. Cover the grill and cook until the flesh of the eggplant is tender, about 15 minutes.

1 small clove garlic

3 to 4 sprigs flat-leaf Italian parsley

1 teaspoon salt

3 tablespoons extra-virgin olive oil

2 large eggplants

Grilled Fruit

Time from start to finish: 20 minutes

2 peaches

2 apricots

5 teaspoons sugar

2 bananas

2 figs

2 plums

SERVES 6 OR MORE

1. Heat a charcoal or gas grill.

2. Prepare the peaches and apricots by cutting each in half, removing the pit, and putting ½ teaspoon sugar on each half. Without peeling the bananas, make a lengthwise incision in each one, but do not cut all the way through. Sprinkle the remaining sugar into the cut. Keep the figs and plums whole.

3. Put the figs, plums, and the bananas, cut side up, on the grill. Turn the figs and plums as they become lightly charred and remove them when they are charred all over. Remove the bananas once the skin side becomes lightly charred and the sugar in the cut has melted.

4. Place the peaches and apricots in a hinged double grill with a handle. Place it over a moderately hot grill with the skin of the fruit facing the fire. When the sugar has melted and the skin becomes slightly charred, turn the grill with the fruit over and cook for 3 to 4 minutes, then remove from the heat. Allow the fruit to settle for a few minutes before serving.

In my early teens, grilling at Nonno David and Nonna Giulia's house in Atlantic Beach.

Chapter 2:

Primi: Soups, Pasta, and Rice

My parents moved back to Italy when I was two, and I grew up as an Italian until we moved back to the States about six years later. When we returned, it was not easy adapting to a new school, a new culture, and a new language—but as my mother writes in her memoir, *Amarcord*, it was not language so much as lunch that was the problem. I could not eat the food at the school cafeteria, so my mother packed lunches for me—though my lunches hardly resembled the peanut-butter-and-jelly sandwiches my classmates brought to school. I have fond memories of the meatballs with tomatoes and peas, the veal stew with mushrooms, and the wonderful soups that my mother would put in a Thermos for me. What I don't have fond memories of is the teasing I endured from my classmates; it embarrassed me so much that I asked my mother to please just pack me a normal sandwich to take to school—not peanut-butter-and-jelly, though, which to this day I cannot imagine eating. My sandwiches were made of cold *frittate* with onions, zucchini, or (my favorite) artichokes, or with a breaded veal cutlet layered with fried eggplant and baked tomatoes. So of course the teasing continued, but I realized that I would rather endure it and eat well. Eventually my lunches were accepted, and perhaps even envied a bit.

Our school had a farm in upstate New York and each class spent a week there every year. It was a fantastic way for city-dwelling kids to learn what it was like to live on a farm. We were all assigned different chores, such as milking the cows or collecting maple syrup, as well as household tasks such as cleaning and cooking. I eagerly looked forward to my turn to cook. I had a quite a hard time with the food that was served, so when it was finally my job to cook, I decided to go all out to make up for it. I called my mother and announced that I wanted to make lasagne for my class and asked her to please tell me how to do it. "Are you sure that's what you want to make?" she said, rather startled. Try as she might, she was not going to dissuade me from my mission. And so it was that—except for the use of store-bought pasta—my first public cooking endeavor was none other than a classic traditional Bolognese lasagne, which, I might add, was very well received!

In addition to lasagne, this chapter includes some of my favorite pasta dishes, such as Al Cantunzein's Pappardelle with Sausage and Peppers (page 82), which I still vividly remember from my teenage days in Bologna with my parents. You will also find the tortelloni filled with Swiss chard (page 73) that my Nonna Mary used to make for me, as well as some of the heartwarming soups my mother used to make when I was growing up.

Cauliflower Soup

Time from start to finish: 45 minutes

My wife didn't really like cauliflower until she met me. Now she loves it, and so do our kids. Cauliflower needs to be cooked until tender to bring out its rich, sweet flavor, which undercooked, still-firm cauliflower never has. It also needs to be seasoned generously to coax its flavor out, but only after it's been boiled. I have found that white vegetables are actually sweeter if they are boiled in unsalted water. This soup is one of the gems I found in a notebook of recipes from my grandmother that my mother has had since she and my father first married. It is now one of our family's favorite soups.

1 cauliflower

8 ounces boiling potatoes (such as Yukon Gold)

3 cups whole milk

Salt

Freshly ground black pepper

3 to 4 sprigs flat-leaf Italian parsley

1 tablespoon butter

SERVES 4

1. Fill a pot large enough to accommodate the cauliflower with water and place over high heat.

2. Remove the leaves from the cauliflower and trim the root. When the water is boiling, add the cauliflower and cook until tender, about 10 minutes.

3. While the cauliflower is cooking, peel the potatoes and cut them into $1/4$-inch slices. When the cauliflower is tender, remove it from the pot and cut the florets away from the root. Discard the water the cauliflower cooked in and put the potatoes, cauliflower florets, and milk in the same pot. Season generously with salt and pepper, cover the pot, and place over medium-high heat. When the milk begins to bubble, reduce the heat to low and cook until the potatoes are tender, about 20 minutes. Keep an eye on the pot during the first few minutes to make sure the milk doesn't boil over; reduce the heat to the lowest setting if necessary.

4. While the soup is cooking, finely chop enough parsley leaves to measure about 1 tablespoon.

5. When the potatoes are done, remove from the heat and pass the soup through a food mill. Add the parsley. Cut the butter into small pieces so it melts more easily, and add to the soup. Stir well and serve at once.

+ **NOTE:** You can prepare the soup several hours ahead of time, but add the parsley and butter just before serving, after reheating the soup.

Homemade Meat Broth

Time from start to finish: 3 hours and 45 minutes

2 medium carrots

1 small tomato

1 medium yellow onion

2 celery stalks

1 small chicken, 3 to 3½ pounds

1 to 1½ pounds veal neck bones
or ribs

4 beef shanks, 3 to 3½ pounds,
or 4 beef marrow bones and about
1½ pounds beef brisket

2 teaspoons whole black
peppercorns

1 tablespoon salt

2 sprigs flat-leaf Italian parsley

4 quarts water

Although it's my mother who still does most of the cooking at my parents' house, there are a few things that have become my father's specialties. A homemade meat broth is one of them. Making homemade meat broth may sound intimidating, but it's actually quite easy, and the rewards are most definitely worth the effort. In addition to having a far superior broth to anything you can buy, you get the added bonus of some of the most succulent and tender meat you can imagine. Serve the meat with a good sea salt and extra virgin olive oil; with horseradish; with a classic green sauce of capers, anchovies, and parsley; or with stewed onions, peppers, and tomatoes.

MAKES ABOUT 4 QUARTS

1. Peel the carrots and the tomato. Peel the onion and cut it in half.

2. Put all the ingredients in a large stockpot. Cover the pot and place over high heat. When the water begins to boil, reduce the heat so that the liquid is simmering very gently. Use a skimmer to remove the scum that rises to the surface. Cook, covered, for 3½ hours.

3. Lift the meats carefully out of the pot. Don't worry if the chicken legs and wings fall off; just scoop them out of the pot. Carve the breast of the chicken and separate the meats from the bones. If using beef brisket, slice it. Store any meat you are not using right away in a container with some of the broth to keep it moist. It will keep for 2 days in a cold refrigerator.

4. Pour the broth through a strainer into a large container, preferably with a spout. Pour the broth into a fat separator. (Pour any unused broth into ice cube trays, place in the freezer overnight, then transfer the broth cubes to a zip-top bag and store in the freezer for up to 2 months.) If you don't have a fat separator, chill the container of broth in the refrigerator, then lift off the layer of fat that will have solidified on the surface with a slotted spatula or spoon.

Minestrone

Time from start to finish: 3 hours and 15 minutes

I must admit I've had a love-hate relationship with this soup. When I was little, I was not very fond of it. When my mother would put it in the Thermos I took to school for lunch, I always wished she had packed the meatballs and stews that I loved so much instead. As I grew older, I began to appreciate the rich, complex flavors of minestrone. When I didn't like something, I was taught to say, "I'm not ready for this yet," rather than "I don't like it." This soup is one of those dishes that I eventually became "ready" for and now enjoy immensely. It's essential to cook it for as long as the recipe specifies to bring out the complexity of its flavor. This is not meant to be a fresh, light spring vegetable soup; it's a soul-warming, restorative soup for cold winter days.

SERVES 4

1. Peel and finely chop the onion. Peel and cut the carrots into ¼-inch dice. Peel the backs of the celery stalks and cut into ¼-inch dice. Put the onion, carrots, celery, olive oil, and butter in a 6-quart soup pot and place over medium-high heat. Sauté until the onion turns a golden color and the carrots and celery just begin to brown, 10 to 15 minutes.

2. While the vegetables are sautéing, finely shred the cabbage. Trim both ends of the green beans and dice them. Peel the potatoes and cut into ½-inch dice. Trim both ends of the zucchini and cut into ½-inch dice.

3. When the onions, carrots, and celery are ready, add the cabbage, season lightly with salt, and cook until the cabbage is wilted, about 5 minutes. Add the green beans, potatoes, and zucchini. Season with salt and pepper, and add the broth or the bouillon cube and 4 cups water and the Parmigiano-Reggiano rind, if using. Once the soup begins to boil, lower the heat to a gentle simmer and cook, covered, for 2½ hours.

4. Add the cannellini beans and cook for another 20 minutes. Serve hot, at room temperature, or with rice as described in the recipe on page 63.

½ medium yellow onion

2 medium carrots

2 celery stalks

3 tablespoons extra-virgin olive oil

2 tablespoons butter

8 ounces Savoy cabbage

4 ounces green beans

12 ounces boiling potatoes (such as Yukon Gold)

12 ounces zucchini

Salt

Freshly ground black pepper

4 cups Homemade Meat Broth (page 60), or ½ beef and ½ chicken bouillon cube

A rind of Parmigiano-Reggiano (optional)

1½ cups canned cannellini beans, drained

Cold Minestrone with Rice

Time from start to finish: 2 hours

3 cups Minestrone (page 61)

3 cups water

¾ cup Italian rice (Carnaroli, Vialone Nano, or Arborio)

12 to 14 fresh basil leaves

4 teaspoons extra-virgin olive oil

When I was in my late teens, my parents opened the School of Classic Italian Cooking in Bologna and I spent a considerable amount of time there. One of the classic Bolognese restaurants we frequented was Diana. As you entered the restaurant, you came upon a large table showcasing the day's specials. Displayed might be luscious, fresh porcini mushrooms, or dishes that were to be served at room temperature. In the summer, one of the latter was a vegetable soup in which rice had been cooked. The term "soup" harkened more to its origins than its current state, since the rice had absorbed most of the broth and the result was almost thick enough to eat with a fork. Drizzled with olive oil and perfumed with fresh basil, what had been the epitome of a winter soup was transformed into a perfect cool summer dish.

SERVES 4

1. Put the minestrone and the water in a 4- to 5-quart pot over high heat. Once the soup is boiling, add the rice, stir well, and reduce the heat to medium. Cook, covered, until the rice is al dente, about 15 minutes. After the rice has cooked for 10 minutes, coarsely shred the basil leaves and add them to the soup.

2. When the rice is done, ladle the soup into serving bowls and allow to cool completely. Serve at room temperature and drizzle about 1 teaspoon of olive oil over each serving.

+ NOTE: You can prepare this a day ahead of time and refrigerate. Take the bowls out of the refrigerator 1 hour before serving to allow to come to room temperature.

Passatelli

Time from start to finish: 15 minutes

½ cup fine dry bread crumbs

1½ cups freshly grated Parmigiano-Reggiano

⅛ teaspoon freshly grated nutmeg

¼ teaspoon salt

Grated zest of ½ lemon (optional)

2 eggs

4 cups Homemade Meat Broth (page 60), or ½ beef and ½ chicken bouillon cube

When I eat this dish, I am immediately transported back to when I was a boy, sitting at my grandmother Nonna Mary's table. Passatelli is one of those dishes that is inextricably tied to the place whence it comes. Romagna (the eastern part of Emilia-Romagna, where my parents were born) is still the only place you'll find this soup. The name literally means "passed through." Dough is pushed, or passed, through a tool that consists of a perforated disk attached to two handles, forming a wormlike shape. You'll only find the tool in Romagna, but a potato ricer is an excellent substitute. Since the broth is an integral part of the soup, I would strongly encourage you to use homemade broth, which is something I always try to have on hand in our freezer. Passatelli are often made with grated lemon zest, which is the way my mother makes them. Personally, I prefer them without, as I find the lemon flavor takes away from the heartwarming earthiness of the dish. I've included it here as an optional ingredient, so you can decide for yourself.

SERVES 4

1. Put all the ingredients except for the broth in a bowl and mix together thoroughly with your hands until a homogeneous dough forms. Let it rest for 5 minutes.

2. Put the broth or the bouillon cube and 4 cups water in a pot and bring to a gentle boil. After the dough has rested 5 minutes, put it through a potato ricer into the boiling broth. Cut off the strands once they are 2 to 3 inches long. After the passatelli rise to the surface, continue cooking for 3 minutes. Serve hot.

Maccheroni Soup with Sausage and Porcini

Time from start to finish: 1 hour

Whenever an idea for a recipe comes to me, I make an entry about it in a notebook. This is one I discovered while leafing through my notes. Unfortunately, I had neglected to include how the idea came to me. It was probably inspired by a soup I ate in Italy, but I don't remember where. Anyway, it turned out so well that it instantly became a favorite with our family. Before I tried this, it had not occurred to me how well porcini and sausage go together!

SERVES 4

1 ounce dried porcini mushrooms

½ medium yellow onion

1 medium carrot

1 celery stalk

3 tablespoons butter

8 ounces mild pork sausage

¾ pound fresh tomatoes

Salt

6 ounces *tubetti* or other short tubular pasta

1. Put the dried porcini in a bowl, add 2 cups water, and soak for at least 15 minutes.

2. Peel and finely chop the onion. Peel the carrot and cut into ⅛-inch dice. Peel the back of the celery stalk and cut into ⅛-inch dice.

3. Put the butter in a 5- to 6-quart soup pot over medium-high heat. When the butter begins to melt, add the onion, carrot, and celery. Sauté until the vegetables begin to brown, about 5 minutes.

4. While the vegetables are sautéing, remove the casing from the sausage and cut into small chunks. Peel the tomatoes and coarsely chop them.

5. When the vegetables are ready, add the sausage. Break up the larger pieces of sausage with a wooden spoon and cook, stirring often, until it loses its raw color, 1 to 2 minutes.

6. Lift the porcini out of the water, squeezing the excess liquid back into the bowl. Do not discard the water. Rinse the porcini under running water, chop them coarsely, and add them to the pot along with the tomatoes. Season lightly with salt and cook, stirring, for about 2 minutes.

7. Add the porcini soaking water to the pot. Be aware that there may be some sand at the bottom of the bowl, so pour carefully or strain through a paper towel. Add 2½ cups water and cover the pot. When the contents come to a boil, reduce the heat to medium and cook for 30 minutes.

8. Add the pasta to the soup. When the pasta is al dente, if there isn't enough broth in the soup, add a little water. Don't add too much, though—the soup should be rather thick. Serve at once.

+ **NOTE:** The soup can be made ahead of time, even the day before. Wait to add and cook the pasta until you are ready to serve.

My father shaving fresh white truffle over risotto for my mother.

Piedmontese Savoy Cabbage and Bean Soup

Time from start to finish: 2 hours

Piedmont is the land of cold and foggy winters, hence the name of the noble grape, Nebbiolo—from *nebbia*, the Italian word for "fog"—that is used to make the famous Barolo and Barbaresco wines. In Italy I find that the foods of a particular region seem to be particularly well paired to the wines of the region. This soup is a perfect example.

SERVES 4

1. Peel and finely chop the onion. Peel and finely chop the garlic. Peel the carrots and cut into ¼-inch dice. Peel the back of the celery stalk and cut into ¼-inch dice. Unravel the pancetta and cut into narrow strips.

2. Put the onion and olive oil in a 4- to 5-quart soup pot over medium-high heat. Sauté until the onion turns a rich golden color, about 5 minutes.

3. While the onion is sautéing, remove the root from the cabbage and finely shred the leaves.

4. When the onion is ready, add the carrots and celery and sauté, stirring, for 1 minute. Add the pancetta and cook until it has lost its raw color, about 1 minute. Add the garlic and cabbage, season with a little salt, and cook, stirring occasionally, for 5 minutes.

5. While the cabbage is sautéing, peel the potatoes and cut in ½-inch dice. After the cabbage has sautéed for 5 minutes, add the potatoes, a little more salt, and a few grindings of fresh pepper. Add the broth or the bouillon cube and 5 cups water and cover the pot. Once the soup begins to bubble, lower the heat to a simmer and cook for 1 hour. While the soup is cooking, finely chop enough parsley leaves to measure about 1 tablespoon.

6. Add the cannellini beans and the parsley. Continue cooking for another 25 minutes, then coarsely shred the basil and add it to the soup. Cook for 5 more minutes. Serve hot.

1 small yellow onion

1 medium clove garlic

2 medium carrots

1 celery stalk

2 ounces pancetta, sliced ¼ inch thick

3 tablespoons extra-virgin olive oil

1 pound Savoy cabbage

Salt

½ pound Yukon Gold potatoes

Freshly ground black pepper

5 cups Homemade Meat Broth (page 60) or ½ beef and ½ chicken bouillon cube

3 to 4 sprigs flat-leaf Italian parsley

1½ cups canned cannellini beans, drained

8 to 10 fresh basil leaves

Egg Pasta of Emilia-Romagna

Time from start to finish: 45 minutes

2¼ cups all-purpose
unbleached flour

3 eggs, at room temperature

FOR GREEN PASTA

8 ounces frozen or 12 ounces
fresh spinach

Making pasta dough by hand is simple. With a little practice, it will become second nature and you will have finished dough in less than 15 minutes. My mother's paternal grandmother, Nonna Polini, made homemade pasta almost every day, rolling it out so thin it was almost transparent—with a rolling pin that was almost as long as she was tall. There are several regions in Italy where homemade pasta is traditionally made, and each recipe is a little different. My family is from Emilia-Romagna, where pasta is made simply with whole eggs and flour. It is impossible to give a precise measurement for the amount of flour needed. Depending on the size of the eggs, the humidity, and even the temperature in the room, you may need more or less. Pasta hates cold temperatures, so don't use eggs straight from the refrigerator, and don't use a cold surface such as marble or stainless steel to knead the dough on. Wood is best. If you do not make perfect pasta dough the first time, don't be discouraged. All you need is a little practice and a pasta machine—just make sure you have some store-bought pasta on hand for dinner the first time around!

SERVES 4

MAKING THE DOUGH

1. Pour the flour in a mound in the center of your work counter. Make a well into which the eggs will fit comfortably. To avoid the possibility that the eggs will overflow, it is better to make the well a little too wide rather than too small.

2. Break the eggs into the center of the well. Use a fork to beat the eggs, until the yolks and the whites are thoroughly blended together. Move a little flour into the eggs and lightly beat with the fork. Continue adding flour until the mixture thickens enough to cling to the fork when you lift it. Set the fork aside, using your fingers to squeeze the dough attached to the fork back onto the counter. Push about ¼ cup flour to the side, then use your hands to bring the rest into the center. Mix together with your hands to begin forming a dough. The dough should feel moist but not sticky when you plunge a finger into it; if it feels sticky, add a little more flour. Wrap the dough in plastic; scrape off any bits of dough that have stuck to the counter and wash your hands. Reserve any remaining flour and set aside.

3. Unwrap the dough and begin kneading it. Think of stretching the dough rather than compressing it, using the heel of your palm and pushing away from you. Knead until the dough feels homogeneous and smooth. If it seems to stick to your hand or the counter, add a little more flour. On the other hand, if it feels too hard to knead, you may have added too much flour. Try wetting your hands and kneading the moisture in. If that does not seem to help, it's probably easier and faster to start over. If you don't need to

add any more flour, kneading should only take 5 to 6 minutes. Adding flour during the kneading process may increase the time, since the farther along you are, the longer it takes for the flour to be incorporated. When you have kneaded the dough sufficiently, wrap it in plastic again and let it rest for at least 15 minutes or up to 3 hours. Never refrigerate or freeze pasta dough. As the dough rests, the gluten in the flour will relax, making it much easier roll the dough.

ROLLING THE DOUGH

1. Unwrap the dough and knead it a few times to incorporate the moisture that will have risen to the surface. The surface of the dough should feel silky smooth (a baby's bottom is what it is traditionally compared to). Cut the dough into as many pieces as you used eggs, in this case, three. Wrap two of the pieces in the plastic wrap. Flatten the remaining piece of dough as best you can with your hands, then put it through the rollers of a pasta machine set at the widest setting. Fold the dough in three, and put it through the rollers again, with the folds perpendicular to the rollers. Fold the dough in half and put it through one more time, again with the folds perpendicular to the rollers. Lay the dough on a dry, lint-free towel and repeat the procedure with the other two pieces.

2. When all the pieces have been through the machine at the widest setting, adjust the rollers down one notch and put each piece of dough through once. Repeat, going down one notch at a time, until you reach the next-to-last setting. Cut each sheet of pasta in half lengthwise, then put each piece through the machine at the thinnest setting.

3. If you are making noodles, let the pasta dry on a cloth until it is leathery in consistency—dry enough that the noodles will not stick together when cut, but still pliable enough that they won't crack. This will take anywhere from 5 to 25 minutes, depending on the temperature and humidity in the room. To cut pasta using the machine, cut the pasta sheets into lengths of 12 to 15 inches. Put each piece through the desired cutting attachment of the machine. Loosely fold the noodles into nests, making them easier to pick up when they are completely dry.

FOR GREEN PASTA

Cook the spinach in salted boiling water until tender. Drain and set aside to cool. When cool, use your hands to squeeze out as much water as possible. Chop the spinach finely by hand or in a food processor, then proceed as instructed in Egg Pasta of Emilia-Romagna, adding the spinach with the eggs, and using an extra $\frac{1}{2}$ cup flour.

My Mother's Butter, Tomato, and Onion Sauce

Time from start to finish: 50 minutes

2 pounds ripe tomatoes, or 3 cups canned whole peeled tomatoes with their juice

1 medium sweet yellow onion

5 tablespoons butter

1¼ teaspoons salt

If I had to pick one dish that exemplifies "Hazan family favorites," it would be this sauce. It is ridiculously simple. You put four ingredients into a pot and place it on the stove. The onion is just peeled and cut in half, no chopping or slicing required. And if you are using canned tomatoes, all you do is open the can, pour it in the pot, and break up the tomatoes with a wooden spoon. But it's not because of how easy it is that it's a favorite; it's because the flavor is addictively delicious. At our cooking school in Italy we offer a "level-two" course for those who want to return for more. I always ask what dish from the first course is their favorite. Out of a week of classes and restaurant meals, the majority say it is this sauce that they remember best. As an added bonus, it can be frozen and will taste just as good when thawed and reheated months later. If you do make a larger batch, be aware that the cooking time will increase.

MAKES ENOUGH FOR 1 POUND DRIED PASTA

1. If using fresh tomatoes, peel them. Coarsely chop the fresh or canned tomatoes. Trim both ends of the onion; peel it and cut it in half lengthwise.

2. Put the tomatoes, onion, butter, and salt in a 4- to 5-quart saucepan over medium heat. When the tomatoes begin to bubble, lower the heat to a slow but steady simmer. Cook, stirring every 10 to 15 minutes, until the tomatoes are no longer watery and the sauce has reduced, about 45 minutes, depending on the size and shape of the pot. The sauce is done when the butter has separated from the tomatoes and there is no remaining liquid.

+ **NOTE:** When you toss pasta with the sauce, add about ⅓ cup freshly grated Parmigiano-Reggiano.

Swiss Chard Tortelloni with Tomato Sauce

Time from start to finish: 1 hour and 45 minutes

I confess I never know what to answer to a reporter's inevitable question: "What is your favorite dish?" It's too hard to choose one! If I really had to, this would probably be it. I am as enamored of these tortelloni today as I was when I was little boy and my grandmother on my mother's side, Nonna Mary, made them for me. I can taste them as I am writing this and can't wait until the next time I make them. While the rest of my family usually requests lasagne on their birthdays, tortelloni would be my request, especially served with the magical tomato sauce on page 72. I like them best when made with Swiss chard, but they are also very good if you substitute spinach.

SERVES 4

1. Make the tomato sauce. It will mostly cook on its own while you work on the rest of the recipe; just remember to stir it once in a while.

2. Remove the stalks from the Swiss chard. Wash the leaves in several changes of cold water and put them in a pot with ½ cup water and 1 teaspoon salt. Place the pot over medium-high heat, cover, and cook until the leaves are tender, 5 to 6 minutes. Drain the leaves and leave them in the colander.

3. Make the pasta dough.

4. Peel and finely chop the onion and put it in a 10-inch skillet with the butter. Place over medium-high heat and sauté until the onion turns a rich golden color, about 5 minutes.

5. While the onion is sautéing, finely chop the prosciutto. Squeeze as much water as possible from the chard and transfer it to a cutting board. Finely chop it. When the onion is ready, add the prosciutto and sauté until it loses its raw, pink color and begins to brown. Add the chard, lower the heat to medium, and sauté for 5 minutes, stirring occasionally. Transfer to a medium bowl and set aside to cool slightly, about 10 minutes.

6. Add the ricotta, ½ cup of the Parmigiano-Reggiano, the egg yolk, and nutmeg to the chard. Season with salt and pepper and stir thoroughly. Taste the filling and adjust the seasoning if necessary.

1 recipe My Mother's Butter, Tomato, and Onion Sauce (page 72)

2 pounds Swiss chard

Salt

1 recipe Egg Pasta of Emilia-Romagna (page 70), made with 2 eggs and 1½ cups flour, dough prepared but not yet rolled

½ medium yellow onion

3 tablespoons butter

2 ounces thinly sliced prosciutto

1 cup whole-milk ricotta cheese

¾ cup freshly grated Parmigiano-Reggiano

1 egg yolk

⅛ teaspoon freshly grated nutmeg

Freshly ground black pepper

¼ cup heavy cream

7. Fill a pot for the pasta with at least 6 quarts water, place over high heat, and bring to a boil.

8. Roll the pasta dough as described on page 70, working with only one piece at a time while keeping the rest of the dough wrapped in plastic. Lay the pasta flat on a cutting board. Place 1-tablespoon dollops of filling at 1-inch intervals along the bottom half of the pasta sheet. Fold the top half of the sheet over the filling and gently press down with your fingers in between all the dollops to squeeze out excess air. Use a pastry-cutting wheel to cut along the bottom edge and the sides, and then in between all the dollops of filling to form approximately 1½-inch squares. The edges will be sealed by the cutting action of the pastry wheel. Place the squares, without overlapping, on a dry cloth. Continue the process with the remaining pasta and filling.

9. Add 2 tablespoons salt to the boiling water. Collect all the tortelloni on one towel and slide them into the boiling water. Cook until the edges are tender, about 5 minutes, then drain or lift them out with a skimmer. Transfer to a shallow serving bowl and gently toss with the sauce and the heavy cream. Sprinkle the remaining Parmigiano-Reggiano over each serving.

Bolognese Meat Sauce

Time from start to finish: 4 hours

∾∾∾∾∾∾∾∾∾∾∾∾∾∾∾∾∾∾∾∾∾∾∾∾∾∾∾∾∾

½ medium yellow onion

1 medium carrot

1 stalk celery

3 tablespoons butter

2 tablespoons extra-virgin olive oil

12 ounces ground beef chuck

½ cup dry white wine

½ cup whole milk

⅛ teaspoon nutmeg

2 cups canned whole peeled tomatoes with their juice

1¼ teaspoons salt

In addition to being a principal component of Bolognese Lasagne, this sauce is so good on its own that it is a staple in our house. It freezes very well, so whenever I make it, I always make enough to last us for three or four meals. Its ideal pairing is with homemade egg pasta (page 70), particularly pappardelle, but it is also wonderful with chewy, substantial shapes of dried flour-and-water pasta such as rigatoni, shells, and cartwheels. It is not at all suited to spaghetti, which does not catch the sauce well. Spaghetti with meat sauce is found in Italian American cuisine but never in Italy.

∾∾∾∾∾∾∾∾∾∾∾∾∾∾∾∾∾∾∾∾∾∾∾∾∾∾∾∾∾

MAKES ENOUGH FOR 1 POUND DRIED PASTA, OR 1 RECIPE EGG PASTA OF EMILIA-ROMAGNA

1. Peel and finely chop the onion. Peel the carrot and celery and cut into ¼-inch dice. Put the onion, carrot, celery, butter, and olive oil in a heavy-bottomed sauce pot over medium-high heat. Sauté, stirring occasionally, until the vegetables are lightly browned, about 10 minutes.

2. Add the ground beef and break it up with a wooden spoon. Add the wine and cook, stirring occasionally, until almost half the liquid has evaporated. Add the milk and nutmeg and cook, stirring occasionally, until half the milk has evaporated.

3. Coarsely chop the tomatoes and add them with their juice to the pot. Add the salt, and once the tomatoes have started bubbling, turn the heat down very low so that the sauce is barely simmering. Cook, uncovered, for 3½ hours, stirring every 15 to 20 minutes. If all the liquid evaporates before the cooking time is up, add water in ½ cup increments, as needed. Make sure all the liquid has evaporated before removing the sauce from the heat.

+ **NOTE:** You can prepare the sauce ahead of time and refrigerate it for up to 3 days or freeze it for up to 2 months.

Béchamel Sauce

Time from start to finish: 20 minutes

In Italian this is called *besciamella*, and the dispute as to whether it was the Italians or the French who invented it will probably never be resolved. It is a white sauce that is quite commonly used in Emilia-Romagna, particularly in baked pasta dishes. It is easy enough that a child can make it (with supervision), and our kids have become quite proficient at it.

2 cups whole milk   *3 cups*
4 tablespoons butter *6*
4 tablespoons flour   *4 ½*
½ teaspoon salt

MAKES ABOUT 2½ CUPS

1. Put the milk in a small saucepan over medium heat. Heat until steam is released when the milk is stirred, just before it boils.

2. While the milk is heating, melt the butter in a 2-quart saucepan over medium–low heat. Add the flour, mixing it in with a whisk until the mixture is smooth. Cook, whisking constantly, for about 1 minute, then remove from the heat. Do not let the flour brown.

3. When the milk is hot, transfer it to a measuring cup or pitcher with a spout. Return the pan with the flour mixture to medium heat and begin adding the hot milk, very slowly at first, mixing with the whisk. Do not be concerned if the mixture becomes quite thick at first. Continue adding the milk slowly while mixing with the whisk. As the consistency becomes thinner, you can add the milk more rapidly until all of it has been mixed in.

4. Add the salt and cook over medium heat, whisking constantly, until the sauce begins to thicken, 10 to 15 minutes. The sauce is done when it coats the whisk thickly. Béchamel is best when used the same day but will keep overnight in the refrigerator if necessary. It's not necessary to reheat it before using.

Bolognese Lasagne

Time from start to finish: 5 hours

1 recipe Bolognese Meat Sauce
(page 76)

1 recipe green or regular Egg Pasta
of Emilia-Romagna (page 70),
dough prepared but not yet rolled

1 recipe Béchamel Sauce (page 77)

Salt

¾ cup freshly grated
Parmigiano-Reggiano

1 tablespoon butter

Lasagne—the Italian plural of *lasagna*, which refers to just one sheet of pasta—is one of our family's favorite foods. Lovingly and carefully made, Italian lasagne bears no resemblance whatsoever to those heavy things that rest in the pit of your stomach for days after being consumed. Bolognese lasagne is a delicate dish that is light, almost airy. It is a savory concoction, with each creamy bite melting in your mouth. It must be made with homemade egg noodles, and there is *NO* ricotta to be found in any of the Hazans' recipes. My father adores green lasagne, and it is what he always requests when we celebrate his birthday at our house. My wife, Lael, who before I met her was quite indifferent to lasagne, now always asks me to make it for her birthday as well.

Lasagne are often judged on how many layers they have. Five or six layers are considered the minimum. For Lael's most recent birthday celebration, I made a spectacular nine-layer lasagne. It was absolutely worth every ounce of effort that went into making it. I have a routine now when I make lasagne, which makes the process fairly easy. I spread the work over two days. The first day I make the Bolognese sauce, which only requires about thirty minutes of my time—because once all the ingredients are in, it cooks on its own. The second day, I begin by making the dough for the pasta; while it rests, I make the béchamel. Then I roll out the pasta, cook it, and assemble the lasagne. The second day's work requires a little over an hour of my time, not counting baking the lasagne.

SERVES 6

1. Make the Bolognese sauce.

2. Make the pasta dough, wrap it in plastic, and set aside to rest.

3. Make the béchamel sauce.

4. When the Bolognese sauce is ready, fill a pot for the pasta with at least 6 quarts water, place over high heat, and bring to a boil.

5. Roll out the pasta dough according to the directions on page 71. Cut the pasta sheets so you have a total of 8 pieces. Fill a large bowl halfway with ice and water and keep it close to the pot of water on the stove.

6. Add 2 tablespoons salt to the boiling water and put in 4 of the pasta sheets. Cook for 1 minute, then lift the pasta out of the water and place it in the bowl of ice water. (I find it easiest to do this with a pair of tongs, but you have to be careful not to rip the pasta.) Swish the pasta sheets in the water, then lay them flat on dry towels. Repeat with the remaining 4 pasta sheets.

7. Preheat the oven to 425°F on the regular bake setting.

8. Spread a thin coating of béchamel on the bottom of an 8-by-11½-inch rectangular baking pan. Mix the remaining béchamel with the Bolognese sauce and ½ cup of the Parmigiano-Reggiano. Use the bottom of the baking dish to determine the length of pasta needed to cover it completely and cut a piece of pasta that you'll use as a template for all the layers. Place a sheet of pasta on the bottom of the pan, filling in with smaller strips any area that the sheet does not cover. Spread a thin coating of the filling over the pasta sheet, then cover with another sheet of pasta. Continue until you have 6 or more layers of pasta and filling, reserving a little filling to cover the top layer. Sprinkle the remaining ¼ cup Parmigiano-Reggiano over the top and dot with pieces of the butter.

9. Bake until the top is lightly browned, 20 to 25 minutes. Take the lasagne out of the oven and let it rest for 5 minutes before serving.

+ **NOTE:** The lasagne can be assembled completely up to 1 day in advance and kept, well wrapped, in the refrigerator. Remove it from the refrigerator 1 hour before baking. It will also keep in the refrigerator after it is baked, for up to 2 days.

Penne with Mushrooms

Time from start to finish: 45 minutes

This is another of the gems I found in my mother's notebook of beloved recipes she inherited from *her* mother. It is one of the first dishes our daughter Gabriella made all by herself from start to finish (I did drain the pasta for her). It is also wonderful with a mixture of shiitake and white mushrooms. In fact, I'm sure it would be good with any assortment of mushrooms. Don't be shy in seasoning this dish. Remember, it's a sauce that is meant to season pasta, so it should be seasoned more aggressively than if it were a stand-alone side dish.

SERVES 4

1. Put the dried porcini in a bowl, cover with water, and soak for at least 15 minutes.

2. Fill a pot for the pasta with about 6 quarts water, place over high heat, and bring to a boil.

3. Brush any dirt off the white mushrooms and thinly slice them. Finely chop enough parsley leaves to measure about 2 tablespoons. Peel and finely chop the garlic.

4. Lift the porcini out of the water, squeezing the excess liquid back into the bowl. Do not discard the water. Rinse the porcini under running water, then chop them coarsely.

5. Put the olive oil, butter, garlic, and parsley in a 12-inch skillet over medium heat. Sauté until the garlic and parsley are sizzling, then add the porcini to the skillet along with the water they soaked in. Be aware that there may be some sand at the bottom of the bowl, so pour carefully or strain through a paper towel. Cook until the porcini water has almost completely evaporated, then add the white mushrooms. Season generously with salt and pepper, cover the pan, and lower the heat to medium. Cook for 10 minutes, stirring approximately every 2 minutes. If the mushrooms begin sticking to the pan before 10 minutes is up, add just a little water.

6. Add 2 tablespoons salt to the boiling pasta water, add the penne, and stir well. Cook until al dente.

7. While the pasta is cooking, add the cream to the sauce and cook until it has reduced enough to thickly coat a spoon. Remove the sauce from the heat. When the pasta is done, drain well, toss with the sauce and the Parmigiano-Reggiano, and serve at once.

1 ounce dried porcini mushrooms

¾ pound white mushrooms

5 to 6 sprigs flat-leaf Italian parsley

2 medium cloves garlic

2 tablespoons extra-virgin olive oil

1 tablespoon butter

Salt

Freshly ground black pepper

1 pound penne

½ cup heavy cream

⅓ cup freshly grated Parmigiano-Reggiano

Al Cantunzein's Pappardelle with Sausage and Peppers

Time from start to finish: 1 hour

2 yellow bell peppers

½ small yellow onion

3 tablespoons extra-virgin olive oil

½ pound plain, mild sausage

Salt

1 pound fresh tomatoes

1 recipe Egg Pasta of Emilia-Romagna (page 70), rolled out thin and cut into wide noodles, or 12 ounces dried store-bought pappardelle, or 1 pound rigatoni or shells

1 tablespoon butter

⅓ cup freshly grated Parmigiano-Reggiano

While I was growing up, pasta was—and it still is—one of my favorite things to eat. When my parents opened their cooking school in Bologna, there was a restaurant called Al Cantunzein (Bolognese for "in the little corner," as it was located in a tiny square near the city center) that would serve course after course of homemade pasta dishes until you told them to stop. I was a teenager with a healthy appetite, and whenever we ate, there I was in heaven. My favorite was green and yellow pappardelle with sausage, peppers, and tomatoes. It is still one of my favorite pasta dishes, especially made with homemade pappardelle, though I usually use only the yellow pappardelle. It is also wonderful with rigatoni or shells. The recipe below, which is almost the same as my mother's in *Essentials of Classic Italian Cooking*, is how I make it now.

SERVES 4

1. Peel the peppers, remove the cores and seeds, and cut into 1-inch squares.

2. Peel and finely chop the onion. Put it with the olive oil in a 12-inch skillet over medium-high heat. Sauté until the onion turns a rich golden color, about 5 minutes.

3. Remove the casing from the sausage. Add the sausage to the skillet and break it into small chunks with a wooden spoon. Once the sausage is lightly browned, 2 to 3 minutes, add the peppers, season lightly with salt, and continue cooking until the peppers are lightly colored, 6 to 8 minutes.

4. While the peppers are cooking, peel and coarsely chop the tomatoes. When the peppers are ready, add the tomatoes to the skillet. Season with salt and continue cooking until the tomatoes are no longer watery, 15 to 20 minutes.

5. While the tomatoes are cooking, fill a pot for the pasta with about 6 quarts of water, place over high heat, and bring to a boil. When the tomatoes are ready and the water is boiling, add 2 tablespoons salt to the pot, drop in the pasta, and stir until all the strands are submerged. Cook until al dente. Drain well, toss with the tomato sauce along with the butter and Parmigiano-Reggiano, and serve at once.

Farfalle with Sausage and Peas

Time from start to finish: 45 minutes

Our older daughter loves peas, so when they are in season we try to use them as much as possible. Although frozen peas are okay, they don't compare with the sensation of spring sweetness you get when you close your mouth around fresh peas. Savory sausage pairs perfectly with peas, and this has become a springtime favorite in our home.

SERVES 4

1. Shell the fresh peas, if using.

2. Fill a pot for the pasta with about 6 quarts of water, place over high heat, and bring to a boil.

3. Peel and finely chop the onion. Put the butter in a 12-inch skillet over medium heat. When the butter begins to melt, add the onion and sauté until it turns a rich golden color, about 5 minutes.

4. While the onion is sautéing, remove the casing from the sausage and cut it into small chunks. When the onion is ready, add the sausage and continue cooking until the sausage has lost all its raw color and begins to brown.

5. Add the peas, season lightly with salt and pepper, stir well, and add 1 cup water. Cover the pan, lower the heat to medium–low, and cook until the peas are quite tender, about 20 minutes (or about 10 minutes if using frozen peas). If all the liquid in the pan evaporates before the peas are done, add a little more water.

6. Add 2 tablespoons salt to the boiling pasta water, add the farfalle, and stir well. Cook until al dente.

7. While the pasta is cooking, add the cream to the sauce and cook until it has reduced and thickly coats a spoon.

8. When the pasta is done, drain well, toss with the sauce and the Parmigiano-Reggiano, and serve at once.

1½ pounds fresh peas in the pod, or 10 ounces frozen peas

½ medium sweet yellow onion

2 tablespoons butter

½ pound mild sausage

Salt

Freshly ground black pepper

1 pound farfalle

½ cup heavy cream

⅓ cup freshly grated Parmigiano-Reggiano

Italian "Mac and Cheese"

Time from start to finish: 25 minutes

Salt

1 pound maccheroni or rigatoni

4 tablespoons butter

¼ cup heavy cream

1 cup freshly grated
Parmigiano-Reggiano

Pasta with butter and cheese: lush, slightly salty, creamy—what's not to like? One of my earliest memories of having it is with my cousin when I was ten or eleven. I remember he was quite serious about how it should be made. "You have to use lots and lots of butter," he pronounced. Michela, our little seven-year-old pasta queen, asked me one day if I knew how to make mac and cheese.

"I make *pasta al burro e formaggio*," I told her.

"OK, I'll tell you how to make it, then," she said. "You need pasta, butter, Parmigiano"—not "cheese," but *Parmigiano*, which made me a very proud papa—"and an orange."

"I see," I said. "Is the orange for color?"

"Yes, but also for flavor," she replied.

It was an intriguing idea—after all, fettuccine with lemon and cream is an inspired combination. On these pages you'll find both the version I've always made and a recipe for fettuccine with orange, as inspired by Michela.

SERVES 4

1. Fill a pot for the pasta with about 6 quarts water, place over high heat, and bring to a boil. Add 2 tablespoons salt to the boiling water, put in the pasta, and stir well. Cook until al dente.

2. While the pasta is cooking, cut the butter into 4 pieces and put it in a serving bowl. Add the cream and 1 teaspoon salt.

3. When the pasta is done, drain well and transfer to the serving bowl. Add half of the Parmigiano-Reggiano and mix thoroughly. Add the remaining cheese, mix well, and serve at once.

Fettuccine with Orange

Time from start to finish: 20 minutes

SERVES 4

1. Fill a pot for the pasta with about 6 quarts water, place over high heat, and bring to a boil.

2. Grate the zest of the orange, taking care not to dig into the white pith. Squeeze enough juice to measure 2 tablespoons.

3. Put the butter in a 10-inch skillet over medium-high heat. When the butter has melted, add the orange zest and juice. Stir for about 1 minute, then add the cream. Add 1 teaspoon salt and a few grindings of pepper, and cook until the cream has reduced by almost half, enough to coat a spoon. Remove from the heat.

4. Add 2 tablespoons salt to the boiling pasta water, put in the fettuccine, and stir until all the strands are submerged. Cook until al dente. When the pasta is done, drain well, toss with the sauce and Parmigiano-Reggiano, and serve at once.

1 orange

3 tablespoons butter

¾ cup heavy cream

Salt

Freshly ground black pepper

1 recipe Egg Pasta of Emilia-Romagna (page 70), rolled out thin and cut into ribbons about ¼ inch wide, or 10 ounces dried store-bought fettucine

⅓ cup freshly grated Parmigiano-Reggiano

My daughter Gabriella cooking in our kitchen.

Fusilli with Peppers and Pancetta

Time from start to finish: 40 minutes

While looking through the refrigerator one day, I noticed a package of multicolored peppers, probably purchased because of their pretty appearance and then forgotten. Further search turned up a thick slice of pancetta and some heavy cream. The ingredients practically screamed out "pasta sauce!" My concoction turned out so well that I added it to my notes for a future book. Since then, I've been making it on a regular basis, so it definitely deserves a place in a book on family favorites. I like cutting the peppers in thin strips. You get more surface area, which means more flavor, and I love the way they wrap around the fusilli.

½ medium yellow onion

½ red bell pepper

½ green bell pepper

½ yellow bell pepper

3 tablespoons butter

¼-inch-thick slice pancetta (about 2 ounces)

Salt

Freshly ground black pepper

1 pound fusilli

½ cup heavy cream

⅓ cup freshly grated Parmigiano-Reggiano

SERVES 4

1. Peel the onion and finely dice it. Peel the peppers using a sawing motion with your peeler and remove the core, seeds, and pith. Cut the peppers in very thin strips.

2. Put the butter in a 12-inch skillet over medium-high heat. When the butter begins to melt, add the onion and sauté until it turns a rich golden color, about 5 minutes.

3. While the onion is sautéing, unravel the pancetta and cut it into thin strips. When the onion is ready, add the pancetta and sauté until it just begins to brown, 2 to 3 minutes.

4. Fill a pot for pasta with about 6 quarts water, cover, and place over high heat.

5. Add the peppers to the skillet and season with salt and pepper. Reduce the heat to medium and cook, stirring often, until the peppers are very tender and lightly colored, about 15 minutes.

6. Add 2 tablespoons salt to the boiling pasta water, add the fusilli, and stir well. Cook until al dente.

7. When the peppers are ready, add the cream and cook until it is reduced by about half, 2 to 3 minutes. When the pasta is done, drain well, toss with the sauce and the Parmigiano-Reggiano, and serve at once.

Ham-and-Cheese *Crespelle*

Time from start to finish: 1 hour and 15 minutes

1 cup whole milk

¾ cup flour

2 large eggs

⅛ teaspoon salt

1 tablespoon butter, or more as needed

½ recipe Béchamel Sauce (page 77)

6 ounces Fontina cheese

6 ounces *prosciutto cotto*, sliced thin (you can substitute a cooked ham that is not too sweet or heavily smoked)

In Italy, where crêpes are called *crespelle*, they are used in baked savory dishes very much like pasta is to make cannelloni. I am a pasta lover at heart, so whenever my mother would make *crespelle*, I always wished it was pasta instead. As I grew older, however, I learned to appreciate *crespelle*. My love for pasta has not waned, but I now enjoy *crespelle* just as much. It may have been our daughters who brought me around. They love making crêpes with a good friend of ours, Gabriela Vigorito, and I discovered I really do like them after all. This is a classic rendition of *crespelle*.

SERVES 4

1. Pour the milk into a mixing bowl. Using a sifter or fine-mesh strainer, slowly add the flour, whisking constantly. Once all the flour is added, continue whisking until the mixture is smooth. Add the eggs and salt and whisk them thoroughly into the batter.

2. Put a thin sliver of the butter in an 8-inch nonstick skillet over medium heat. Once the butter has melted completely, add 3 tablespoons of the batter. Pick up the skillet and tilt it in a circular motion to spread the batter evenly over the bottom. Cook until the sides of the *crespella* begin to lift from the pan and the bottom is speckled brown, about 1½ minutes. Using a spatula, turn the *crespella* over and continue cooking until the other side is also speckled brown, about 30 seconds, then transfer it to a plate. Add another thin sliver of butter to the skillet and repeat the procedure until all the batter has been used. The *crespelle* can be stacked on the plate; they won't stick together.

3. Make the béchamel.

4. Preheat the oven to 425°F on the bake setting.

5. Assemble the *crespelle*. Grate the Fontina using the large holes of a grater. Smear a thin coating of the béchamel on a baking dish. Place one *crespella* on a clean plate and coat it with some of the béchamel. Cover with a slice of the *prosciutto cotto* (no larger than the *crespella*) and sprinkle some of the cheese on top. Roll the *crespella* loosely and place in the baking dish. Continue until all the *crespelle* have been used. Use the remaining béchamel to coat the top of the *crespelle*.

6. Bake the *crespelle* for 8 to 10 minutes, until the tops just begins to brown. If they don't begin to brown after 10 minutes, place them briefly under the broiler. Serve hot.

Nonna Giulia's Rice

Time from start to finish: 30 minutes

½ red bell pepper

½ green bell pepper

½ pound tomatoes

2 tablespoons vegetable oil

1½ cups short- or medium-grain rice

1 teaspoon salt

One of the foods I looked forward to the most when we would have Friday night Shabbat dinners with my grandparents David and Giulia was this rice dish, which was always part of our meal. It was comforting, filling, and flavorful. I loved the bits of pepper and tomato and made sure I got some in every bite. When I tried to re-create it for my family, I made the mistake at first of putting in too many of those tasty bits I loved. It simply reaffirmed the fact that sometimes too much of a good thing ends up not being good anymore. I remember my grandmother's rice was fluffy and soft and shorter than typical long-grain rice, but you can easily make this with other varieties of rice as well.

SERVES 4

1. Peel the bell peppers and cut into ¼-inch dice. Peel the tomatoes, remove the seeds, and cut the flesh into ¼-inch dice.

2. Put the oil in a 4-quart saucepan over medium-high heat. As soon as the oil is hot, add the rice and stir until it is well coated. Add 2½ cups water, the bell peppers, tomatoes, and salt. Cover the pan, and once the water begins bubbling, lower the heat to medium and cook for 20 minutes, without stirring. Serve hot.

Nonna Mary's White Rice

Time from start to finish: 30 minutes

This is the rice my mother's mother, Nonna Mary, used to make. She called it *riso pilaf*, but unlike most rice pilaf recipes, this is a plain white rice. It cooks in the oven and comes out perfectly every time. You'll need a pot that can go from the stovetop to the oven. Enameled cast iron is an ideal choice.

1 tablespoon butter

1 cup white rice

1½ cups water

½ teaspoon salt

SERVES 4 AS A SIDE DISH

1. Preheat the oven to 350°F on the bake setting.

2. Put the butter in a 1½-quart ovenproof pot over medium-high heat. When the butter has melted, add the rice and stir until it is well coated. Add the water and salt.

3. When the water begins to bubble, cover the pot and place in the oven. Bake for 20 minutes. Remove from the oven and let stand, covered, for 2 to 3 minutes before serving.

I am two years old with Nonna Mary in Cesenatico.

Piedmontese Rice and Fontina

Time from start to finish: 30 minutes

4 tablespoons butter

1½ cups Italian rice (Carnaroli, Vialone Nano, or Arborio)

2¼ cups water

1 teaspoon salt

2 ounces Fontina cheese

Here is an incredibly easy dish whose luscious flavor is dependent on the ingredients used. Val d'Aosta is actually a separate region bordering Piedmont to the north, and it includes the Italian slope of Monte Bianco (Mont Blanc). The cheese for which it is famous, Fontina, gets its distinctive flavor from the milk produced by cows that graze on mountain grasses and wildflowers at close to 6,000 feet. The rice should be the special short-grained rice used for risotto that Piedmont is known for—in particular Carnaroli, which is considered the prince of risotto rices.

SERVES 4

1. Preheat the oven to 350°F on the bake setting.

2. Put 1 tablespoon of the butter in an ovenproof pot that has a lid and place over medium-high heat. When the butter has melted, add the rice and stir until it is well coated. Add the water and salt. Once the water begins to bubble and the oven is hot, place the covered pot in the oven and bake for 20 minutes.

3. While the rice is cooking, grate the Fontina using the large holes of a grater. Cut the remaining butter into small pieces and put in a serving bowl.

4. When the rice is done, transfer it to the serving bowl and stir until the butter has melted. Add half the grated cheese, stir well, then stir in the remaining cheese. Serve hot.

Risotto with Eggplant

Time from start to finish: 45 minutes

One of the dishes I often teach is *Spaghetti alla Norma*, a classic Sicilian pasta made with eggplant and tomato and finished with mozzarella cheese. One day, I had some eggplant and tomatoes left over and it occurred to me that they would make a good risotto. I eliminated the mozzarella because I didn't think it would work with the creaminess of risotto. I was quite surprised with how well it turned out. The eggplant practically dissolves in the end, becoming a delicate, creamy accompaniment to the rice. A rustic pasta dish was transformed into an elegant, delicious risotto.

½ medium yellow onion

3 tablespoons extra-virgin olive oil

1 medium clove garlic

1 pound fresh tomatoes

Salt

1 pound eggplant

1¾ cups rice for risotto (Carnaroli, Vialone Nano, or Arborio)

12 to 14 fresh basil leaves

SERVES 4

1. Peel and finely chop the onion. Put it with 2 tablespoons of the olive oil in a 5- to 6-quart braising pan over medium-high heat. Sauté until the onion turns a rich golden color, about 5 minutes.

2. While the onion is sautéing, peel and finely chop the garlic. Peel and coarsely chop the tomatoes. When the onion is ready, add the garlic, sauté for about 30 seconds, then add the tomatoes. Season lightly with salt, reduce the heat to medium, and cook for a few minutes, the time it takes to prep the eggplant in the next step.

3. While the tomato is cooking, peel the eggplant and cut into ³/₄-inch chunks. Add the eggplant to the pan and season lightly with salt. Cover the pan and cook until the eggplant becomes translucent, 8 to 10 minutes.

4. While the eggplant is cooking, put 2 quarts water in a pot over high heat. When it begins to boil, reduce the heat to low.

5. When the eggplant is ready, uncover the pan, raise the heat to medium-high, and add the rice. Stir until it is well coated, then add about 1 cup of the hot water and continue stirring. Add only enough water to produce the consistency of a rather thick soup and wait until all the liquid is absorbed before adding more. Continue until the rice is al dente, 18 to 20 minutes. After 10 minutes, coarsely chop the basil and add it to the pan

6. Remove the risotto from the heat and stir in the remaining tablespoon olive oil. Serve at once.

Risotto with a Mushroom Medley

Time from start to finish: 45 minutes

One of the foods our family always looks forward to when we go to Italy is wild mushrooms, especially fresh porcini. The combination of flavor and texture is rich and sensual. Back home, fresh porcini are pretty hard to get, especially in Florida. There are plenty of other varieties of wild mushrooms available in the States, however. One day we unexpectedly received a wonderful assortment of wild mushrooms, which I used to make this fantastic risotto. I would encourage you to try this with different combinations of mushrooms, such as shiitake and chanterelles.

SERVES 4

1. The hen of the woods and beech mushrooms only need to have their roots removed. The oyster mushrooms and most other mushrooms should be sliced.

2. Peel and finely chop the onion. Put it with the olive oil in a 5- to 6-quart heavy-bottomed braising pan over medium-high heat. Sauté until the onion turns a rich golden color, about 5 minutes.

3. While the onion is sautéing, peel and finely chop the garlic. Finely chop enough parsley leaves to measure about 2 tablespoons. When the onion is ready, add the garlic and parsley and sauté for 30 seconds. Add all the mushrooms and season with salt and pepper. Add ½ cup water and cook until all the liquid evaporates and the mushrooms are tender and lightly browned, about 10 minutes.

4. While the mushrooms are cooking, put the broth or the bouillon cube and 5 cups water in a pot over high heat and bring to a boil, then lower the heat to maintain a very gentle simmer.

5. When the mushrooms are ready, add the rice and stir until it is well coated. Add about 1 cup of the hot broth and continue stirring. Add only enough broth to produce the consistency of a rather thick soup and wait until all the liquid is absorbed before adding more. Continue until the rice is al dente, 18 to 20 minutes. Remove the risotto from the heat, add the butter, stir well, and serve at once.

12 ounces assorted wild mushrooms (hen of the woods, beech, oyster, or other)

½ medium yellow onion

3 tablespoons extra-virgin olive oil

1 large clove garlic

5 to 6 sprigs flat-leaf Italian parsley

Salt

Freshly ground black pepper

5 cups Homemade Meat Broth (page 60) or ½ beef and ½ chicken bouillon cube

1¾ cups rice for risotto (Carnaroli, Vialone Nano, or Arborio)

1 tablespoon butter

Risotto with Pesto

Time from start to finish: 30 minutes

1 medium clove garlic

¾ cup fresh basil leaves
(you'll need a bunch of basil
weighing about 1 ounce)

¼ cup pine nuts

5 tablespoons extra-virgin olive oil

1½ teaspoons salt

½ medium yellow onion

1¾ cups rice for risotto
(Carnaroli, Vialone Nano,
or Arborio)

Our girls adore basil pesto. We once rented an apartment in Liguria in order to explore the foods of the region, and the girls happily ordered pasta with pesto at almost every single meal. When I am lucky enough to have a nice bunch of basil in our vegetable garden, I make a large batch of pesto and freeze it in individual portions. One day, rather than having it with pasta, I decided to stir it into a basic risotto, and we were delighted with the results. The natural creaminess of risotto carries the aromatic flavor of pesto perfectly. I've held back the cheese in this version to keep it lighter and fresher.

SERVES 4

1. Peel the garlic and cut it in half. Put one half in a food processor along with the basil leaves, pine nuts, 3 tablespoons of the olive oil, and ½ teaspoon of the salt. Run the processor until a fine, creamy mixture forms. Set the pesto aside.

2. Put about 6 cups water and the remaining teaspoon of salt in a saucepan over medium-low heat.

3. Peel and very finely chop the yellow onion. Put it with the remaining 2 tablespoons olive oil in a 5- to 6-quart braising pan over medium-high heat. Sauté until the onion turns a rich golden color, about 5 minutes.

4. While the onion is sautéing, finely chop the remaining half clove of garlic. When the onion is ready, add the garlic, sauté for another minute, then add the rice. Stir until it is well coated, then add about 1 cup of the hot water from the saucepan and continue stirring. Add only enough liquid to produce the consistency of a rather thick soup and wait until all the liquid is absorbed before adding more. Continue until the rice is al dente, 18 to 20 minutes. Remove from the heat, stir in the pesto, and serve at once.

Risotto with Fresh Tomatoes, Peas, and Porcini

Time from start to finish: about 1 hour

1 ounce dried porcini mushrooms

1½ pounds fresh peas in the pod, or 10 ounces frozen peas

½ medium yellow onion

3 tablespoons butter

1 pound fresh tomatoes

Salt

Freshly ground black pepper

1¾ cups rice for risotto (Carnaroli, Vialone Nano, or Arborio)

We always bring dried porcini back home from Italy. Their quality is much better than what we usually find in the States, and they easily keep for a year. Often I'll make a risotto using only dried porcini. When I had some fresh tomatoes and peas on hand, it occurred to me that they would go very well with the woodsy flavor of dried porcini, and we were not disappointed—the experiment has now become a family favorite.

SERVES 4

1. Put the dried porcini in a bowl, cover with water, and soak for at least 15 minutes.

2. Shell the peas if using fresh. Peel and finely chop the onion. Put the onion in a 5- to 6-quart braising pan with 2 tablespoons of the butter over medium-high heat. Sauté until the onion turns a rich golden color, about 5 minutes.

3. While the onion is sautéing, peel and coarsely chop the tomatoes. Lift the porcini out of the water, squeezing the excess liquid back into the bowl. Do not discard the water. Rinse the mushrooms under running water, then chop them coarsely. When the onion is ready, add the porcini, the tomatoes, and the fresh or frozen peas. Season with salt and pepper, add 1 cup of water, and cook, covered, until the peas are tender, about 15 minutes if using fresh or less than 10 minutes if using frozen.

4. Transfer the porcini water to a saucepan, pouring it through a strainer lined with a paper towel, and place over medium-low heat. Put about 6 cups water in another saucepan over medium-low heat as well.

5. When the peas are ready, uncover and raise the heat to medium-high. If there is still liquid in the pan, let it evaporate, then add the rice and stir until it is well coated. Add about 1 cup of the hot porcini water and continue stirring. Add only enough liquid to produce the consistency of a rather thick soup and wait until all the liquid is absorbed before adding more. Continue cooking until the rice is al dente, 18 to 20 minutes, using plain water once the porcini water is all used up. Remove from the heat and stir in the remaining tablespoon of butter. Serve at once.

My father, Victor, making risotto.

My daughter Gabriella in front of original seventeenth-century pestles still used to process rice for risotto.

Chapter 3:

Secondi: Meats and Seafood

Nonno Fin was my grandfather on my mother's side; his name was actually Giuseppe, but everyone called him Fin. He passed away when I was only six or seven. Though I do not remember much from that time, I do have a few very clear memories of Nonno Fin. I remember how he had a little seat that fit onto the handlebars of his bicycle and how he would take me around Cesenatico, proudly showing off his grandson. I loved those outings and eagerly looked forward to them.

Cesenatico was, and is still is, a beautiful beach town and fishing village. It has a major wholesale fish auction house that operates as a reverse auction: For each lot, the price starts high and goes down until someone places a bid. Buyers must decide whether to wait to bid—and risk losing the lot of fish—or bid sooner at a higher price to be sure to get it. Bidding requires a great deal of experience, and seats at the auction house are passed on from generation to generation.

Nonno Fin usually stayed out of the kitchen, which was my grandmother's domain, except when fish was involved. He was the one in charge of fish, from buying it at the *pescheria*, the retail fish market in the center of town, to carefully cleaning it, and finally cooking it. His preferred method was on the grill. His grill was actually just a metal bassinet with a grill on top in which he would put charcoal. It resided on the terrace of the second floor of my grandparents' house, and he made my grandmother rather nervous whenever he lit it. He would grill small fish with a reddish hue—similar to red mullet but smaller—called *triglie* in Italian, or *barboncini* in the local dialect. He would also grill *saraghine*, a member of the herring family, whose closest equivalent is a sprat, a little fish slightly larger than an anchovy but smaller than a sardine—in fact, *saraghine* are often mistaken for baby sardines. Nonno Fin taught me how to eat both of these fish: *con il bacio*, "with a kiss." You grab the fish by its head and its tail, as you would an ear of corn, and suck the sweet flesh from the spine, first on one side and then on the other. Both the *saraghine* and the *barboncini* were so fresh and sweet that all he cooked them with was salt.

Many years later, my wife and I were in Cesenatico with our two young daughters, ages four and eight at the time. One of the few things our older daughter, Gabriella, did not eat at that time was fish, probably from having been served fish sticks at a school lunch. We were at a favorite fish restaurant and discovered that they had fresh *saraghine*. I immediately ordered some and they arrived steaming hot, on the grill they had been cooked on. I breathed in their rich aroma as I picked one up and began eating it like Nonno Fin had taught me to. I was in heaven. Gabriella, always the adventurous eater, saw the effect the *saraghine* had on me and decided to try one. Her days of not eating fish were instantly over, and we ended up ordering two more portions.

Nonno Fin did not limit himself to grilling. Another of his specialties was mackerel (I suppose it must be from Nonno Fin that I inherited my particular fondness for blue fishes). He would pan roast it with olive oil, garlic, and rosemary. His most famous dish, however, was *il brodetto*, a fish soup that was a masterful symphony of flavors.

Nonna Mary, my grandmother on my mother's side, was an excellent cook. Many of the dishes I've learned from my mother are ones that Nonna Mary used to make. Her undisputed specialty was frying. In fact, the only time that Nonno Fin would let Nonna Mary handle fish was when it involved frying. Anything Nonna Mary fried was incredibly light and pure; I can still taste the sweet, delicate flavor of her fried Adriatic sole. She was also a fearless fryer.

My mother often told me how during the war, if my grandmother was in the middle of frying something, even air-raid sirens would not stop her until each perfect morsel was out of the pan.

Frying also became one of my mother's specialties. From my mother I learned how expertly fried food is neither heavy nor greasy. Frying forms a crisp, protective shell that preserves the flavor of what you are frying, delivering its essence to your palate. A perfect example is fried custard cream, an item that is always part of a traditional Bolognese *fritto misto*. As unusual as it may seem, custard is delicious when lightly breaded and fried. The combination of its crisp exterior with its luscious, sweet, creamy interior creates an extraordinary sensation on the palate. My mother could fry almost anything, and I never grew tired of watching her, absorbing her technique as if by osmosis. I loved her fried veal cutlet, especially paired with her fried eggplant, which she made without any batter or coating. It was one of the few things she fried that was not crisp; it was a sweet essence of eggplant that melted in your mouth. Another of my favorites was the zucchini she fried after dipping it in *pastella*, a simple flour-and-water batter.

I used to love helping her make the *pastella*. I would whisk as she slowly added flour to a bowl of water. I was supposed to tell her when just the right amount of flour had been added. She would correct me if I told her to stop too soon, or if I waited too long. Eventually I was right every time, and I think I've inherited the frying gene. When we celebrate Hanukkah, Lael, my wife, prepares the mixture but it's always my duty to fry the latkes. Whenever we are in Italy in late spring and we see zucchini and squash blossoms, my kids beg me to fry them, pulling out the big-eyes-head-cocked-to-one-side puppy look they have perfected. "We'll help!" they entreat. It reminds me of how my father used to bat his eyes, imploring my mother to make *calamaretti fritti*—tiny fried squid—for him, and she would always give in, notwithstanding the prospect of the inevitable oil-splatter cleanup. So now it's my daughters who whisk as I add the flour, learning to tell when the batter is the perfect consistency.

Chicken with a Lemon Inside

Time from start to finish: 1 hour and 45 minutes

1 whole chicken, about 3½ pounds

Salt

1 lemon

Freshly ground black pepper

This is probably one of my mother's most famous dishes. She has heard from so many people who have made this chicken when they proposed that it's been dubbed "engagement chicken." It makes a regular appearance on our family table. Few recipes are this simple, and except for turning the chicken once, kids can do almost everything else. If you are using a different size chicken, figure on a total cooking time of approximately 25 minutes per pound.

SERVES 4

1. Preheat the oven to 350°F on the regular bake setting.

2. Rinse the chicken inside and out and pat it dry. Sprinkle some salt inside the cavity.

3. Wash the lemon and roll it on the counter, pressing down to crush the inside without breaking the rind. Use a toothpick to puncture the lemon in at least 20 places. Put the lemon inside the chicken and close the cavity using one or more toothpicks. Turn the chicken breast side up and sprinkle all over with salt and pepper. Place the chicken, breast side down, in a roasting pan, preferably with a grate on the bottom. Sprinkle again with salt and pepper.

4. Bake the chicken for 30 minutes (or one-third of the total cooking time), then turn it breast side up and bake for another 30 minutes. If you have a convection even, change the oven setting to convection heat and raise the temperature to 400°F, or to 425°F in an oven without convection heat. After another 30 minutes, remove the chicken from the oven and let it rest for 2 to 3 minutes.

5. Transfer the chicken to a cutting board, preferably one that has grooves along the edges to catch the juices as you carve. Cut away the legs at the thigh joint and remove the wings. Slice the breast and place it along with the dark meat in a serving dish. Remove the grate from the roasting pan and pour the juices the chicken has released back into the roasting pan. Put the pan over medium–high heat. Loosen the browned bits at the bottom of the pan with a wooden spoon and let the sauce reduce until it is thick enough to coat the spoon. If there was not enough juice from the chicken, add a little water. Pour the sauce over the chicken in the serving dish and serve at once.

+ **NOTE:** If the chicken is rather fatty, you may need to use a ladle to skim the excess fat from the sauce before pouring it over the chicken.

Grilled Marinated Chicken Breasts

Time from start to finish: 1 hour

The problem with chicken breasts is that they go rather quickly from underdone to overcooked and dried out. Marinating them with lemon solves the problem. The lemon juice actually begins the cooking process while the chicken marinates, thereby reducing time on the grill and producing moist, white meat. This is a dish I like to make when we have friends over for a casual meal. I marinate the chicken early in the day and take it out of the refrigerator about 20 minutes before putting it on the grill. Together with a nice big mixed salad, this makes for a great summer weekend meal.

1½ pounds boneless, skinless chicken breasts

3 medium cloves garlic

1 sprig fresh rosemary

¼ cup freshly squeezed lemon juice

2 tablespoons extra-virgin olive oil

Salt

Freshly ground black pepper

SERVES 4

1. Lay the chicken breasts in a shallow baking dish large enough to accommodate them without overlapping. Peel and lightly crush the garlic. Cut the rosemary sprig into 3 pieces. Distribute the rosemary and garlic around the chicken pieces. Add the lemon juice and olive oil and season with salt and pepper. Turn the chicken pieces over and let stand at room temperature for about 45 minutes, or in the refrigerator for at least 2 hours.

2. Heat the grill until it is very hot. Put the chicken breasts on the grill and cook for 8 minutes. Turn the chicken over and pour the marinade over it. Cook until done, 6 to 8 more minutes, depending on how thick the pieces are. Transfer to a clean serving platter and serve hot.

Chicken Breasts with Tomatoes, Capers, and Olives

Time from start to finish: about 35 minutes

½ small yellow onion

1 pound fresh, ripe tomatoes, or 1 cup canned whole peeled tomatoes with their juice

1 pound boneless, skinless chicken breasts

2 tablespoons extra-virgin olive oil

Salt

Freshly ground black pepper

3 sprigs fresh oregano

12 black olives

1 tablespoon capers

When I was growing up my mother used to make thin sliced beef steaks she called *alla pizzaiola*, because the sauce was reminiscent of a popular pizza topping: tomatoes, capers, olives, and oregano. You are not likely to find chicken in my parents' house, as my father is not fond of fowl, but I've discovered the sauce is a perfect accompaniment for chicken breast fillets.

SERVES 4

1. Peel and finely chop the onion. If using fresh tomatoes, peel them and coarsely chop them. If using canned, coarsely chop them.

2. Slice the chicken breasts horizontally into 2 or 3 thin fillets. Put the olive oil in a skillet over medium-high heat. When the oil is quite hot and makes a corner of a chicken fillet sizzle, carefully slide in as many chicken fillets as will comfortably fit. When they have browned on one side, turn them over and brown the other side, then transfer them to a platter. If the chicken is stuck to the pan when you try to turn it, just wait a little longer. Don't try to pull it off the pan or you'll tear it. Once all the chicken is done, season it with salt and pepper.

3. Remove the skillet from the heat and add the onion. There should be enough residual heat to make it sizzle. Once the sizzing begins to subside, place the skillet over medium heat and sauté the onion until it softens and turns a caramel color, 2 to 3 minutes. When the onion is ready, add the tomatoes and season lightly with salt. Cook until the tomatoes have reduced and are no longer watery—at least 10 minutes. If all the liquid evaporates before they have cooked for 10 minutes, add a little water.

4. While the tomatoes are cooking, coarsely chop enough oregano leaves to measure about 1½ teaspoons. Slice the flesh of the olives away from the pits (or simply slice them lengthwise if already pitted). Once the tomatoes have cooked for 5 minutes, add the oregano. When the tomatoes are ready, add the olives and capers, stir well, then put the chicken fillets back in the pan. Turn the chicken in the sauce, and when the fillets are heated through, remove from the heat and serve at once.

Photo-Shoot Chicken

Time from start to finish: 1 hour and 15 minutes

My mother did not make chicken very often because it is one of the few things my father doesn't like. She loves chicken, however, so occasionally she'd make something else for my father and chicken for us. I loved the braised chicken she made, usually with peppers, onions, and tomatoes. This dish was inspired by what remained after a photo shoot in our house. Zucchini, peppers, tomatoes, and onions had been purchased to create an attractive still life, and they needed to be used, so "photo-shoot chicken" was born. I cooked it in the typical Italian fashion, braised in a pan over the stove. I used the whole chicken cut up into pieces, as we all like both dark and white meat. The trick to getting moist breast meat is simple: Cook it less than the dark meat. I wait to add it to the pan until the dark meat has cooked for twenty-five minutes; that way in the end you get fall-off-the-bone-tender dark meat and moist white meat.

1 small sweet yellow onion

1 medium zucchini (10 ounces)

1 green bell pepper

1 yellow bell pepper

1 pound fresh tomatoes

1 whole chicken, 3½ to 4 pounds

2 tablespoons extra-virgin olive oil

Salt

Freshly ground black pepper

SERVES 4

1. Peel and thinly slice the onion crosswise. Cut the ends off the zucchini, then slice it in quarters lengthwise, then into ½-inch chunks. Peel the bell peppers using a sawing motion with a peeler, then remove the cores and pith and cut into ¾-inch squares. Peel the tomatoes the same way and coarsely chop them. Keep the onions separate and put all the other vegetables in a bowl.

2. Cut the chicken into 12 pieces—2 drumsticks, 2 thighs, 2 wings, the breast into quarters, and the back in halves. The back flavors the sauce, and the bits of meat on it are very tasty.

3. Choose a braising pan that holds the chicken pieces snugly, put in the olive oil, and place over medium-high heat. When the oil is quite hot, add half the chicken pieces and brown them lightly on both sides. Transfer the pieces to a platter and repeat with the remaining chicken. Once all the chicken is browned and on the platter, season with salt and pepper.

4. Remove the pan from the heat and add the onion and a light sprinkling of salt. Once the sizzling of the onions subsides, put the pan back over medium heat. Sauté until the onion turns a rich golden color, 8 to 10 minutes.

5. Add all the vegetables and tomatoes and season them lightly with salt. Put all the chicken except for the breast meat back into the pan along with any juices it has released. Cover the pan with the lid slightly askew and cook for 25 minutes, turning the chicken pieces once halfway through. Add the breast pieces and continue cooking with the lid askew for another 20 minutes. Turn the chicken pieces again at least once during this time. If there is no more liquid in the pan before the chicken is ready, add a little water. In the end, the vegetables will have become very tender, almost a sauce. If the contents of the pan are still rather watery when the chicken is done, raise the heat and cook, uncovered, until the sauce has thickened. Serve hot.

+   **NOTE:** The chicken may be prepared ahead of time and will keep very well for 1 to 2 days.

With my wife, our daughters, and our dog, Truffle.

Lamb Braised with Peppers

Time from start to finish: 2 hours

Braised dishes are great for when schedules are crazy around dinnertime. Eating individually and on the run is just not part of our family's lifestyle. Sharing meals as a family is something we treasure, so when there isn't time to prepare a meal, having a braised dish like this one that just needs reheating fits the bill perfectly. I like using a combination of peppers, because the tart green pepper balances the sweet flavor of the red and yellow ones. Peeling the peppers not only removes tough skin, but it also makes them taste richer and sweeter by eliminating the skin's bitter flavor.

SERVES 4

1. Peel the garlic cloves and put them with the olive oil in a 5-quart braising pan. Place over medium-high heat. Lightly brown the garlic on all sides, then remove it from the pan.

2. Add as many lamb chops as will comfortably fit in the pan and brown them lightly on both sides. Transfer the chops to a plate and season with salt and pepper. Repeat until all the lamb is done.

3. While the lamb is browning, coarsely chop enough sage to measure 2 teaspoons. Chop enough rosemary leaves to measure 2 teaspoons. When all the lamb is out of the pan, add the herbs, stir for about 15 seconds, and add the white wine. Let it bubble away for about a minute to evaporate the alcohol, while you loosen the browned bits on the bottom of the pan with a wooden spoon.

4. Put the lamb and any juices it has released back into the pan, lower the heat to a steady simmer, about medium heat, and cover the pan, with the lid slightly askew. Cook until the lamb is tender, 1 hour and 15 minutes to 1 hour and 30 minutes, turning the lamb every 15 to 20 minutes. If all the liquid in the pan evaporates before the lamb is tender, start adding ½ cup water at a time until the meat is done.

5. While the lamb is cooking, peel the peppers, remove the cores and seeds, and cut into pieces approximately 1 inch by ½ inch. When the lamb chops are tender, add the peppers, season lightly with salt, and cook, covered, until the peppers are quite tender, about 15 minutes. Serve hot.

2 cloves garlic

2 tablespoons extra-virgin olive oil

3 pounds lamb shoulder chops

Salt

Freshly ground black pepper

8 to 10 fresh sage leaves

1 sprig fresh rosemary

⅓ cup dry white wine

1 green bell pepper

1 red bell pepper

1 yellow bell pepper

Fried Parmesan Cheese–Battered Lamb Chops

Time from start to finish: 25 minutes

12 lamb rib chops, about 2¼ pounds

2 eggs

½ cup freshly grated Parmigiano-Reggiano

⅓ cup fine dry bread crumbs

Vegetable oil

Salt

Freshly ground black pepper

To celebrate our wedding anniversary, my parents had us over for a special luncheon. On the menu were fried lamb chops, which I had not had for a very long time. In fact, not since I was still living at home in New York. Apartments in New York do not lend themselves to barbecue grills, unless you are fortunate enough to have a terrace, which we didn't. So when we had lamb chops, my mother would fry them in a Parmesan batter. They were crispy, savory, and decadently delicious. The next time our family was in the mood for lamb chops at home, I decided to make my mother's fried chops, and they have now become one of our family's favorites as well. The rib chops must be pounded fairly thin so that the meat will cook before the batter becomes burnt. Don't make them too thin, however, or you'll end up with more batter than meat. I like them rather meaty, close to a half-inch thick, and I fry them over medium heat so the chops are cooked but still pink in the center by the time the batter is nicely browned. My recipe is almost the same as my mother's, with minor variations in quantities and method.

SERVES 4

1. Pound the eye of each lamb chop until it is just under ½ inch thick.

2. Put the eggs in a small bowl and whisk until the yolks and whites are thoroughly mixed together. Put the grated cheese and bread crumbs in two separate bowls.

3. Holding one of the chops by the bone, coat the eye of the chop in the grated cheese, dip it in the egg mixture, letting all the excess drip back into the bowl, then coat it with the bread crumbs, shaking off the excess. Repeat with the remaining chops.

4. Put enough vegetable oil in a 10-inch skillet to come ¼ inch up the sides. Place over medium heat. When the oil is hot enough to make a corner of a chop sizzle, put as many chops in the skillet as will fit comfortably. Cook until a nice brown crust forms, about 1½ minutes, then turn the chops and cook until the other side is also nicely browned. Transfer the chops to a platter lined with paper towels and add more chops until they are all done. Season both sides of the chops with salt and pepper and serve at once.

Boeuf Giuliano

Time from start to finish: 2 to 2½ hours

2 carrots

4 ounces cipolline onions, or pearl onions

2 ounces pancetta, sliced ⅛ inch thick

2 tablespoons butter

1 tablespoon vegetable oil

3 pounds short ribs

Salt

Freshly ground black pepper

½ cup full-bodied dry red wine

After I saw *Julie & Julia*, my mouth was watering for boeuf bourguignon. Instead of making Julia Child's recipe, I came up with a more Italian-style dish that I couldn't help naming "Boeuf Giuliano." It is actually quite similar to a *brasato di manzo*, a braised beef dish that my maternal grandmother used to make. Instead of the traditional beef chuck, I decided to make it with some short ribs that looked particularly good at the market, and I was very pleased with the results.

SERVES 4

1. Peel the carrots and cut them into ½-inch chunks. Peel the onions. If using cipolline, cut them in half; leave pearl onions whole. Unravel the pancetta and cut into narrow strips.

2. Put the butter and vegetable oil in a braising pan over medium–high heat. When the oil and butter are quite hot and the butter is just beginning to change color, put the short ribs in and brown them on all sides. When they are done, transfer them to a platter and season with salt and pepper.

3. Add the carrots, onions, and pancetta to the pan and sauté, stirring, for about 1 minute. Add the red wine and let it bubble away for about 30 seconds to allow the alcohol to evaporate. Put the short ribs back in the pan, lower the heat to a steady simmer, and cover the pot, with the lid slightly askew. Cook until the meat is very tender, 1½ to 2 hours, turning the ribs every 20 minutes. If all the liquid in the pan evaporates before the ribs are tender, add ½ cup water at a time until the meat is done. Serve hot, with some good crusty bread.

+ **NOTE:** This dish will be very good the next day too. Reheat it gently in the pan with a little bit of water.

Lael's Meatloaf

Time from start to finish: 50 minutes

Though this recipe is not from my side of the family, it is undoubtedly one of our family's favorites. It's a dish that our girls always look forward to when I'm traveling. Fortunately, my wife, Lael, also makes it when I'm home. It has all the qualities of our favorite dishes: simplicity, ease of preparation, and genuine flavors. Usually, Lael uses a mixture of beef and pork, but sometimes she likes making it with equal parts of beef, pork, and veal. This is probably the first recipe I have ever written that calls for ketchup, but it just wouldn't be the same without it.

SERVES 4

1. Preheat the oven to 350°F on the regular bake setting.

2. Put all the ingredients in a mixing bowl and combine thoroughly with your hands.

3. Place the mixture into a 1¾-quart baking dish approximately 3 inches deep and bake for 30 minutes. Raise the heat to 400°F on the convection bake setting, or to 425°F for an oven without convection heat. Bake for another 15 minutes. Serve hot.

1 pound ground beef chuck

½ pound ground pork

1 egg

½ teaspoon fresh rosemary

⅛ teaspoon dried thyme

⅛ teaspoon dried sage

¼ teaspoon dried marjoram

2 tablespoons ketchup

¼ cup fine dry bread crumbs

¼ cup whole milk

1 teaspoon salt

Freshly ground black pepper

My wife, Lael, with our daughter Michela in Cinque Terre, Italy.

Meatballs with Tomatoes and Peas

Time from start to finish: 1 hour

1 slice plain white bread

2 tablespoons whole milk

½ small yellow onion

1 pound ground beef chuck

1 egg

¼ cup freshly grated
Parmigiano-Reggiano

⅛ teaspoon freshly grated nutmeg

Salt

Freshly ground black pepper

¼ cup fine, dry bread crumbs

Vegetable oil

1 cup canned whole peeled
tomatoes with their juice

1¼ pounds fresh peas in the pod,
or 8 ounces frozen peas

These meatballs go a long way back. I remember my grandmother Nonna Mary would make them and serve them with her version of rice pilaf (page 93), which she prepared in the oven. They were also a staple in my parents' house, and one of my favorite items that my mother would pack in a Thermos for my lunch at school. They continue to be a staple in our current household, where we make them at least once a month. They keep perfectly when frozen, so I usually make a large batch. To reheat them, place them in saucepan with a couple tablespoons of water over medium-low heat. I've also discovered that they can be made into a great pasta sauce. When I reheat them, I break them up into small bits and add a tablespoon of butter and a pinch of salt. I like them with the same pasta I would use for the Bolognese meat sauce, chunky shapes like rigatoni or shells, or egg pasta such as tagliatelle or pappardelle. Add about ¼ cup of freshly grated Parmigiano-Reggiano when you toss the pasta.

SERVES 4 (MAKES ABOUT 20 MEATBALLS)

1. Cut away the crust from the slice of bread. Put it in a small bowl and pour the milk over it.

2. Peel and finely chop the onion. Put it in a large bowl with the ground meat, egg, Parmigiano–Reggiano, and nutmeg. Mash the bread and milk to a pulp with your fingers and add it to the bowl. Season with 1 teaspoon salt and a few grindings from the pepper mill. Thoroughly mix everything together with your hands.

3. Put the bread crumbs in a small, shallow bowl. Form the meat mixture into small compact meatballs, about 1½ inches in diameter, and roll each meatball in the bread crumbs until coated on all sides.

4. Put enough oil in a 10-inch skillet to come ¼ inch up the sides and place over medium–high heat. When the oil is hot, carefully add about half of the meatballs. Lightly brown them on all sides; remove from the skillet and set aside. Repeat with the remaining meatballs.

5. Pour off most of the oil from the pan, leaving just enough to coat the bottom. Return the pan to medium heat and add the tomatoes, breaking them into small pieces with a wooden spoon. Lightly season the tomatoes with salt, then return all of the meatballs to the pan. Cover the pan, with the lid slightly askew, and adjust the heat so that the tomatoes simmer.

6. If using fresh peas, shell them. Add the fresh peas after the meatballs have cooked for 20 minutes and continue cooking for 20 more minutes, or add the frozen peas after the meatballs have cooked for 30 minutes and continue cooking for 10 more minutes. If all the liquid in the pan evaporates before the meatballs are ready, begin adding ½ cup water at a time until they are done. Serve hot, with good crusty bread or Nonna Mary's Rice (page 93).

At eight years old, learning to fish from Nonno David.

Tagliata with Garlic and Parsley

Time from start to finish: 25 minutes

1 medium clove garlic

5 to 6 springs flat-leaf Italian parsley

Sea salt

Freshly ground black pepper

2 boneless rib-eye steaks (about 2½ pounds total weight), cut 1¼ inches thick

4 tablespoons extra-virgin olive oil

Our family enjoys a thick rib-eye from time to time. Using this cut makes it possible to get a nice crust formed while keeping the inside rare and tender, something you can't easily do with a thin steak. A 1¼-inch-thick steak can weigh over a pound, though, and that's much more meat than one of us can consume. In Italy, steak is usually served sliced and we call it *tagliata*, meaning "cut." Slicing it allows you to toss the meat, after it is grilled, with hot olive oil and herbs, making it even more delicious. We like to vary the herbs we use. Sometimes I simply heat the olive oil with whole garlic cloves and rosemary sprigs, then discard them and briefly toss the meat in the pan with the flavored olive oil. In the recipe below, I barely sizzle chopped garlic and parsley in olive oil, then toss the meat in it. Of course, an excellent extra-virgin olive oil will make all the difference.

SERVES 4

1. Preheat a charcoal or gas grill.

2. Peel and finely chop the garlic. Finely chop enough parsley leaves to measure about 2 tablespoons.

3. Generously sprinkle sea salt and black pepper on both sides of the steaks. Grill for about 5 minutes on each side for rare steak, bearing in mind that after it is sliced, the meat will be briefly exposed to heat in the skillet.

4. Put the garlic, parsley, and olive oil in a large skillet. Place over medium-high heat and sauté until the garlic begins to sizzle, then reduce the heat to low.

5. While the garlic and parsley are sautéing, transfer the steaks to a cutting board and cut on a bias into ¼-inch slices. After you have reduced the heat under the skillet to low, add the sliced steak and toss until it is well coated. Serve at once.

Uccellini Scappati

Time from start to finish: 40 minutes

"Escaped little birds" is what the name of this dish means in Italian. I'm not really sure why, but that is what they were called in my mother's little notebook, in which she wrote my grandmother Nonna Mary's recipes. This dish is partly responsible for launching my mother's career. It's what she made when she invited famous *New York Times* food editor Craig Claiborne to lunch. My mother had submitted information on the cooking classes she had just started offering for inclusion in the *Times*' listing, but unfortunately she missed the deadline. At the time, there really wasn't anyone else teaching authentic Italian cuisine, and Claiborne was intrigued. My mother prepared a full multicourse Italian meal for him, with these veal rolls as the second course. She assumed that they would sit down to eat as soon as he arrived, so when the doorman announced that Mr. Claiborne was on his way up, she put the fully cooked rolls back on the stove to reheat. However, Claiborne wanted to interview my mother first, so my mother rushed to remove the veal rolls from the heat. After the interview, she placed them back on the stove and they sat down to eat the appetizer and first course. The doorman called again, saying the photographer was now on his way up. Off the heat went the veal rolls again. It was a comedy of errors but, miraculously, the veal rolls held up, and the rest is history!

1 pound veal scaloppine, thinly sliced

4 ounces prosciutto, thinly sliced

¼ cup freshly grated Parmigiano-Reggiano

2 tablespoons butter

1 tablespoon vegetable oil

¼ cup dry white wine

¾ cup canned whole peeled tomatoes with their juice

Salt

Freshly ground black pepper

SERVES 4

1. Lightly pound the veal scaloppine. Cover each scaloppina with a slice of prosciutto and sprinkle 1 teaspoon of the Parmigiano–Reggiano on top. Roll the meat up like a jelly roll and secure it with a toothpick.

2. Put the butter and vegetable oil in a 12-inch skillet over medium-high heat. When the oil and butter are quite hot and the butter is just beginning to change color, place the veal rolls in the skillet in a single layer and brown them on all sides. Transfer the rolls to a platter.

3. Add the wine to the pan and let it bubble for about 30 seconds to allow the alcohol to evaporate. Add the canned tomatoes and break them up with a spoon. Season with salt, lower the heat to medium, and cook, covered, for 15 minutes. Season the veal rolls on the platter with salt and pepper.

4. After the tomatoes have cooked for 15 minutes, put the veal rolls back in the pan and heat, covered, for 2 to 3 minutes, until they are cooked through. Serve hot.

Veal Cutlets

Time from start to finish: 15 minutes

1 egg

¾ cup fine dry bread crumbs

1½ pounds veal scaloppine, about
¼ inch thick

Vegetable oil

Salt

Probably the best sandwich my mother made for me to take to school was a *cotoletta di vitello*, a breaded veal cutlet that tasted just as good cold as it did hot, together with fried eggplant and sometimes a bit of oven-baked tomatoes (page 39).

SERVES 4

1. Break the egg into a small bowl and whisk until the yolk and white are evenly mixed.

2. Spread the bread crumbs on a plate. Dip the veal into the egg, let the excess drip back into the bowl, then place the veal on the plate with the bread crumbs, coating it well on both sides. Repeat until all the veal is done.

3. Put enough vegetable oil in a skillet to come ¼ inch up the sides and place over medium-high heat. When the oil is hot enough to sizzle the corner of a scaloppina, put as many slices of veal in the skillet as will comfortably fit without overlapping. After they have browned on one side, 1 to 2 minutes, turn the scaloppine and brown the other side, 1 to 2 minutes. Remove from the heat, sprinkle with salt, and serve either hot or at room temperature.

At my home serving
my parents the
green lasagne
I made for my
father's birthday.

Veal Scaloppine with Black Truffles

Time from start to finish: 20 minutes

Sadly for our bank accounts, everyone in our family adores truffles. Whenever I go to Italy without my family, the thing our daughter Gabriella wants me to bring back the most is tubes of white truffle paste. On a recent trip, I did even better; a good friend of ours gave me a gift of fresh black and white truffles. Our kids were in heaven, and we had truffles for three meals in a row on my return. The delicate flavor of veal turned out to be a perfect vehicle for the blalck truffles' rich, woodsy aroma.

1 pound veal scaloppine, sliced thin

About ½ cup all-purpose flour

1 tablespoon vegetable oil, or more if needed

2 tablespoons butter

Salt

Freshly ground black pepper

1 (2- to 3-ounce) fresh black truffle

SERVES 4

1. Pound the veal.

2. Spread the flour on a small plate. Put the oil and 1 tablespoon of the butter in a large skillet over medium–high heat. While the oil and butter are heating, coat with the flour as many slices of veal as will comfortably fit in the pan, shaking off the excess. Do not dredge all the veal in the flour at once or it will become soggy.

3. When the oil and butter are quite hot, and the butter is just beginning to change color, place the coated veal slices in the pan. When they have lightly browned on both sides and lost their raw, pink color, less than 1 minute per side, remove them, letting the excess oil drip back into the skillet, and set them aside on a platter. Flour and cook the remaining veal in the same manner. If the pan becomes too dry, add a little more oil when the pan is empty, and let it get hot before continuing. When all the scaloppine are done, season them with salt and pepper.

4. If there is more than a light coating of oil left in the pan, pour it out. Pour any juices that the meat on the platter has released into the skillet and add enough water so that there is about ⅛ inch of liquid in the pan. Use a wooden spoon to loosen the browned bits on the bottom of the skillet and let the liquid bubble away until it has reduced and thickened into a sauce, 1 to 2 minutes.

5. Add the remaining tablespoon of butter and remove the pan from the heat. Stir the butter into the sauce, then put the scaloppine back into the pan, turning each one in the sauce to heat through.

6. Place the scaloppine on a serving platter large enough to accommodate them in a single layer and pour the sauce over them. Use a truffle slicer or vegetable peeler to slice the truffle into thin shavings over the scaloppine. Serve at once.

Mahshi

Time from start to finish: 1 hour and 30 minutes

2 heads Savoy cabbage

Salt

½ medium yellow onion

5 to 6 sprigs flat-leaf Italian parsley

1 pound ground lamb
(if unavailable, substitute
1 pound ground beef)

½ cup Italian rice for risotto
(Carnaroli, Vialone Nano, or
Arborio)

Freshly ground black pepper

2 medium cloves garlic

2 tablespoons butter

3 tablespoons extra-virgin olive oil

½ cup freshly squeezed lemon juice
(2 lemons)

My maternal grandmother's family were Italian expatriates who had settled in the Middle East. Nonna Mary was born in Beirut and lived in Egypt for a while. One of the dishes I remember her making, which she had learned in Egypt, was *mahshi*, a traditional Middle Eastern dish of cabbage rolls filled with rice and ground meat. They were a wonderful treat when she served them, and when I started working on this book, I asked my mother if she remembered how Nonna Mary used to make them. "Of course!" she replied, and she pulled out an old notebook, stained and worn, in which she had written down some of my grandmother's recipes when she married my father and found herself needing to cook for him. Amazingly, my mother let me borrow her treasured notebook, and soon I was cooking Nonna Mary's *mahshi* at home. As my wife and our girls first sat down to eat them, I could almost see Nonna Mary sitting right next to us. I think she would have approved!

SERVES 4

1. Place a pot filled with 4 quarts water over high heat. Cover and bring to a boil.

2. Carefully remove the cabbage leaves, taking care not to break them. Stop once the leaves become smaller than 4 inches wide. You should end up with about 24 leaves.

3. When the water is boiling, add 1 tablespoon salt and the cabbage leaves. Cook until the leaves are just tender, about 8 minutes. Lift them out of the water and lay them on a platter to cool.

4. While the cabbage is cooking and cooling, prepare the meat-and-rice filling. Peel and finely chop the onion. Finely chop enough parsley leaves to measure about 2 tablespoons. Put the ground meat, rice, onion, and parsley in a mixing bowl. Season with salt and pepper and mix thoroughly with your hands.

5. When the cabbage leaves are cool enough to handle, cut away the portion of each rib that is wider than ¼ inch. Lay a cabbage leaf flat, take a ball of the filling about 1½ inches in diameter, roll it between your palms to form a little sausage, and place it on the cabbage leaf. Roll the leaf up with the filling inside, folding in the edges as you go along. Gently squeeze out any excess moisture and place the roll in a 12-inch skillet. Continue until you have used up all the filling, or all the leaves. The rolls can be quite snug and even overlap a bit in the skillet. If you have filling left over, you can crumble it and add it to the skillet.

6. Peel and coarsely chop the garlic and add it to the skillet along with the butter, olive oil, and lemon juice. Add enough water to come ¼ inch up the sides, place over medium-high heat, and cover the pan.

7. Once the liquid in the pan begins to bubble, lower the heat to medium-low and cook for 40 minutes. Check the *mahshi* occasionally but do not turn them. If all the liquid has evaporated before they are done, add a little more water. In the end there should be very little liquid left. If there is too much, remove the cover and raise the heat until it has evaporated. Serve hot.

With my daughters Michela (right) and Gabriella (left) in Valpolicella, Italy.

Stuffed Zucchini

Time from start to finish: 1 hour and 15 minutes

3 pounds zucchini

½ pound ground beef chuck

¾ cup Italian rice for risotto (Carnaroli, Vialone Nano, or Arborio)

⅛ teaspoon freshly grated nutmeg

Salt

Freshly ground black pepper

1½ pounds fresh tomatoes, or 1½ cups canned whole peeled tomatoes with their juice

1 medium clove garlic

2 tablespoons extra-virgin olive oil

This dish is a perfect example of the amazing convergence of both sides of my family's roots. My paternal grandmother, Nonna Giulia, and my maternal grandmother, Nonna Mary, both made these stuffed zucchini almost exactly the same way. Unfortunately, I have no written record from either grandmother, so my recollection has morphed into a single recipe. The tricky part is hollowing out the zucchini without breaking through the skin. The easiest way is to scoop from both ends of the zucchini, then push the insides out. The pulp is not used here but can be made into a delicious pasta sauce or used in a frittata.

SERVES 4

1. Cut off the ends of the zucchini, then cut each squash in half crosswise. Use an apple corer (or a dinner knife with a rounded tip) to scoop out the inside of each zucchini, leaving a tube shape with a ¼-inch wall. Save the pulp for another meal.

2. Put the ground beef and rice in a mixing bowl. Add the grated nutmeg and season with salt and pepper. Mix well with your hands, then fill the hollowed-out zucchini with the mixture. Only fill up to about ¼ inch from the ends to allow space for the rice to expand as it cooks.

3. Peel and coarsely chop the tomatoes.

4. Peel and finely chop the garlic and put it with the olive oil in a shallow braising pan or a skillet deep enough to accommodate the zucchini. Place the skillet over medium-high heat. When the garlic begins to sizzle, add the tomatoes and season lightly with salt.

5. Once the tomatoes are bubbling, add the stuffed zucchini, lower the heat to medium, and cook until very tender, 45 to 50 minutes. If there is still liquid in the pan when they are done, raise the heat and cook, uncovered, until the sauce reduces. Serve hot or at room temperature.

Italian Baby Back Ribs

Time from start to finish: 1 hour and 45 minutes

The combination of meat with sweet flavors is completely foreign to an Italian palate. I confess that when I was a boy and had my first encounter with barbecue sauce, I was quite taken aback. In fact, I still have not learned to like cranberry sauce with turkey or mint jelly with lamb. You may not think that ribs are an Italian dish, but they are definitely part of Northern Italy's culinary repertoire, especially in the region around the Dolomites and the northern Veneto. So if you are in the mood for ribs and want to try something different, here's a recipe for succulent baby back ribs braised with tomato and sage. In the unlikely event you have leftovers, you can make an excellent pasta sauce: Remove the meat from the bones (it will practically fall off by itself), cut it up and mix it with the sauce, and serve with a sturdy pasta shape such as rigatoni or maccheroni.

1 full rack of pork baby back ribs (about 3 pounds)

2 tablespoons extra virgin olive oil

Salt

Freshly ground black pepper

1 medium clove garlic

6 large fresh sage leaves

⅓ cup dry white wine

3 tablespoons red wine vinegar

2 cups canned whole peeled tomatoes with their juice

SERVES 4

1. Cut the rack into individual ribs. Put the olive oil in a braising pan that will accommodate the ribs snugly (some overlap is fine). Place the pan over medium-high heat. When the oil is hot, put the ribs in and brown them on all sides. Transfer the ribs to a plate and season with salt and pepper. Remove the pan from the heat.

2. While the ribs are browning, peel and finely chop the garlic. Coarsely chop the sage leaves.

3. After removing the pan from the heat, add the garlic and sage and stir for about 15 seconds. Return the pan to medium-high heat and add the wine. Let it bubble for about 30 seconds to allow the alcohol to evaporate, then add the vinegar. Let the vinegar bubble for 30 seconds, then add the canned tomatoes, breaking them into small pieces with a wooden spoon. Season the tomatoes with salt, and put the ribs back into the pan. Once the tomatoes are bubbling, lower the heat to medium-low and cover the pan, with the lid slightly askew. Cook until the ribs are very, very tender, 1 hour and 15 minutes to 1 hour and 30 minutes, turning them every 20 minutes. If all the liquid in the pan evaporates before the ribs are ready, add some water. If the sauce is too liquid when the ribs are done, remove the cover, raise the heat, and reduce the sauce. Serve hot, with good crusty bread.

Veal Stew with Mushrooms

Time from start to finish: 2 hours

1½ pounds boneless veal shoulder,
or about 2¼ pounds shoulder chops

½ medium yellow onion

2 tablespoons butter

1 tablespoon vegetable oil

Salt

Freshly ground black pepper

8 to 10 fresh sage leaves

¼ cup dry white wine

¾ pound white mushrooms

½ cup heavy cream

This is another of those dishes I remember my mother putting in my Thermos for my school lunch. Veal, mushrooms, and cream go particularly well together, especially when served with rice. Prepackaged "veal stew" meat always seems suspect to me, so I buy either boneless veal shoulder or shoulder chops and then cut the meat into chunks myself. Taking a little extra time to trim away any tough membranes and excessive fat ensures that you'll have tender, succulent veal. If you have a hard time obtaining veal, beef chuck will also work very well here.

SERVES 4

1. Cut the veal into 1½-inch chunks. Peel and finely chop the onion.

2. Put the butter and oil in a 5-quart braising pan over medium-high heat. When the oil and butter are quite hot and the butter is just beginning to change color, add half the veal. Brown it on both sides and transfer to a platter. Repeat with the remaining veal. Once it is all browned, season it with salt and pepper.

3. Add the onion to the pan and sauté until it is lightly browned and begins to soften, about 3 minutes. While the onion is sautéing, coarsely chop enough sage to measure about 2 teaspoons and add it to the pan.

4. When the onion is ready, add the wine and let it bubble for about 30 seconds to allow the alcohol to evaporate. Put the meat back in the pan, along with any juices it will have released. Lower the heat to a steady simmer, and cover the pan, with the lid slightly askew. Cook for 1 hour, stirring every 15 to 20 minutes. If all the liquid in the pan evaporates, add a little more water.

5. While the veal is cooking, brush any dirt off of the mushrooms and cut them into ½-inch chunks. After the meat has cooked for 1 hour, add the mushrooms, season lightly with salt and pepper, and continue cooking, with the lid askew, until the veal is very tender, but at least 30 more minutes, stirring occasionally.

6. Raise the heat to medium-high and allow any liquid in the pan to evaporate. Add the cream and cook until it has reduced enough to thickly coat a spoon. Serve hot, with some crusty bread or white rice.

Animelle Croccanti
(Giuliano's Crisp Sweetbreads)

Time from start to finish: 1 hour and 45 minutes

Though most people would probably not think of serving sweetbreads to their kids, ours can't get enough of these. They are crisp and salty on the outside, tender and sweet on the inside, and this makes them very appealing. Perhaps the trick is not to dwell on what they actually are. Although it is a bit time-consuming to remove all the membranes, it is worth it. Sweetbreads have a delicate flavor, savory with a hint of sweet, and their texture is firm, not mushy. It's hard to eat just one bite!

1 pound sweetbreads

½ cup all-purpose flour

3 tablespoons butter

Salt

SERVES 4

1. Soak the sweetbreads in cold water for 1 hour.

2. Fill a pot large enough to hold the sweetbreads with water and place over high heat.

3. Using a paring knife, carefully remove all membranes and gristle from the sweetbreads. When the water in the pot is boiling, add the sweetbreads and cook for 20 minutes. Remove the sweetbreads from the pot and check for any remaining membranes.

4. Pat the sweetbreads dry with a paper towel and roll them in the flour, shaking off the excess.

5. Put the butter in a 10-inch skillet over medium-high heat. When the butter foam begins to subside and the butter just begins to brown, add as many floured sweetbreads as will comfortably fit in the pan. When they are lightly browned on one side, after 2 to 3 minutes, turn them over. When lightly browned on both sides, transfer to a platter lined with a paper towel. When all the sweetbreads are done, sprinkle with salt and serve at once.

Fried Seafood *alla Romagnola*

Time from start to finish: 20 to 25 minutes

1½ pounds squid, medium shrimp, scallops, or fillet of sole, or an assortment

¾ cup all-purpose flour

Vegetable oil

Salt

Cesenatico, the town on the Adriatic where my mother was born, makes most Italians think of summer vacations at the beach, but it is also one of the major fishing villages on the coast. I have sweet memories of carefree summers spent in Cesenatico while growing up, but the sweetest may be of the flavor of its seafood. Just thinking about it makes me hungry—the *calamaretti fritti*, tiny fried squid you pop into your mouth whole; the tender baby cuttlefish; the fresh, intensely flavored shrimp; and the delicacy of Adriatic sole, probably the finest sole in the world. When seafood is fried in Cesenatico, it's to highlight its flavor, so it's never fried in heavy batters or dipped in sauces. One of our favorite restaurants specializing in fried seafood goes so far as to implore its customers not to "ruin their fried seafood" by asking for lemon. Although we may not be able to get those same delicate creatures here, there is certainly some fine seafood to be had in the States, and this is my favorite way to fry it.

SERVES 4

1. If using squid, wash them, removing any guts and the thin bone inside the sac. If there is still a gray membrane on the outside of the sac, peel it away. If using shrimp, peel and devein them. If using scallops, remove the tough tendon, if still attached. Scallops should be cut in half, or in quarters if they are very large.

2. Pat the seafood dry with paper towels. If using sole, spread the flour on a plate and coat both sides of the fish, shaking off the excess. Otherwise, put a handful of the seafood in a fine-mesh strainer, place it over a bowl, and pour enough flour over the seafood to coat it well. Shake the strainer until all the excess flour falls into the bowl. Continue until all the seafood is coated with flour. It's fine to reuse the flour that collects in the bowl, if needed.

3. Put enough oil in a 10-inch skillet to come ½ inch up the sides and place over medium-high or high heat—the oil should be hot enough for there to be a lively sizzle when the seafood is frying, but not so hot that the food begins to burn in less than a minute. When the oil feels quite hot when you hold your hand a couple of inches above it, test a piece of seafood in it. If the piece sizzles immediately, the oil is hot enough. Add as much seafood as will comfortably fit in the pan. (It's better to do several batches than to overcrowd the pan.) If frying shrimp or sole fillets, turn them after 1 minute. Squid and scallops do not need to be turned. Any of these items should be done in less than 2 minutes. When the surface turns to a golden color, the seafood is ready. Lift it with a slotted spatula, letting excess oil drip back into the pan, and place on a platter lined with paper towels. Sprinkle with salt and serve at once.

With my wife and daughters in Liguria, Italy.

Grilled Sea Scallops with a Parsley-Thyme Sauce

Time from start to finish: 25 minutes

2 tablespoons fresh lemon juice

Salt

7 to 8 sprigs flat-leaf Italian parsley

3 to 4 sprigs fresh thyme

5 tablespoons extra-virgin olive oil

1½ pounds sea scallops

Freshly ground black pepper

2 to 3 tablespoons fine dry bread crumbs

Skewers for grilling

Occasionally, my father will go into the kitchen and prepare one of his specialties. One of these is a fragrant fresh-thyme sauce he pairs with grilled salmon. When I came across some beautiful fresh diver scallops at our favorite fish market, it occurred to me that my father's sauce would be great with grilled scallops. Sweet and delectable, scallops are particularly well suited to grilling, which creates a rich, caramelized crust while keeping the inside tender and moist, and the thyme sauce was indeed a perfect accompaniment.

SERVES 4

1. Preheat a charcoal or gas grill.

2. Put the lemon juice with 1 teaspoon salt in a small bowl. With a small whisk or a fork, mix thoroughly until the salt has dissolved. Chop enough parsley leaves to measure about 2 tablespoons and enough thyme leaves to measure about 2 teaspoons. Add the parsley and thyme to the bowl. Add 4 tablespoons of the olive oil and whisk until emulsified.

3. Put the remaining olive oil in a separate bowl. Add the scallops, season with salt and pepper, and toss until coated with the oil. Add the bread crumbs and toss again. Thread the scallops onto two parallel skewers (this prevents them from spinning around).

4. Place the skewers on the grill and cook until firm and cooked through, 2 to 3 minutes on each side, depending on how large the scallops are. Transfer to a serving platter and serve with the parsley-thyme sauce on the side.

Il Brodetto, My Version

Time from start to finish: 50 minutes

My maternal grandfather's specialty was preparing fish, particularly his fish soup. On the Adriatic coast, where my family is from, it is known as *brodetto*, whereas on the Mediterranean side it is called *cacciucco*. The idea is the same: a delicate yet richly flavored assortment of fish and seafood in a tomato broth, born of fishermen's need to utilize unsold fish. Its rich, sweet flavor came from stewing fish heads, then extracting the tasty morsels of flesh to add to the broth. In *Essentials of Classic Italian Cooking*, you'll find my mother's recipe, which faithfully reproduces my grandfather's famous *brodetto*. It calls for cooking three or four fish heads in the base, then removing all the flesh with your hands and pureeing it back into the pot. When I am not in the mood to embark on such a project, or I am not able to get fish heads, I use the shells of the shrimp (or whichever crustacean you are using) to give it a richness of flavor instead. I cook them in the base only briefly, or my *brodetto* would end up tasting more like a bouillabaisse. My recipe also uses fish fillets, which is how most fish is sold in the States, rather than whole fish. To make it quicker and simpler, I don't use squid, which require lengthy cooking to be tender, and because I like the lighter flavor this soup has without them. You can use any assortment of fish that does not include sole, because it is too bland, or mackerel and other blue fishes, because they are too strongly flavored. In addition to or instead of the shrimp, you can use rock shrimp or lobster. I use mussels but not clams, which I find are usually too tough. If you can get small, tender steamers, they would go very well here. Even though I've ended up changing my grandfather's dish quite a bit, each bite still vividly reminds me of him.

½ small yellow onion

1 medium clove garlic

⅛ teaspoon red pepper flakes

3 tablespoons extra-virgin olive oil

5 to 6 sprigs flat-leaf Italian parsley

⅓ cup dry white wine

1 cup canned whole peeled tomatoes with their juice

Salt

½ pound extra-large shrimp, rock shrimp, or lobster tail

¾ pound mussels

1½ pounds mild, firm-fleshed fish (such as red snapper, grouper, striped bass, or halibut)

½ pound sea scallops

4 thick slices good crusty bread

SERVES 4

1. Peel and finely chop the onion. Peel and finely chop the garlic. Put the onion, garlic, red pepper flakes, and olive oil in a 5-quart braising pan over medium-high heat. Sauté until the onion turns a rich golden color, about 5 minutes.

2. While the onion is sautéing, finely chop enough parsley leaves to measure about 2 tablespoons.

3. When the onion is ready, add the wine and let it bubble for about 30 seconds to let the alcohol evaporate. Add the canned tomatoes, season lightly with salt, and break them up into small chunks with a spoon or spatula. Reduce the heat to medium, add the parsley, and cook until the tomatoes have reduced and are no longer watery, about 10 minutes.

4. While the tomatoes are cooking, shell and devein the shrimp or lobster tail, if using. Try to keep the shells whole as much as possible; set them aside.

5. When the tomatoes are done, add 1½ cups water and the shrimp or lobster shells. Cover the pan and cook for 15 minutes, then remove from the heat. You can prepare the *brodetto* up to this point several hours ahead of time.

6. When you are ready to serve, remove the shells, scraping as much of the tomato as possible back into the pan. Wash the mussels in several changes of cold water until you do not see any more sand. Discard any that are open. Place the pan over medium-high heat. When the contents begin bubbling, add the fish fillets and season them with salt. Cover and cook for 5 minutes, then turn the fish and add the mussels, shrimp, and scallops. Season the shellfish with salt and cover the pan again. Cook until the mussels have opened and the shrimp have turned pink, 3 to 5 minutes.

7. While the seafood is cooking, toast or grill the bread and place a slice in each soup bowl in which you are serving the *brodetto*. As soon as the shellfish is done, pour the *brodetto* over the toasted bread and serve at once.

At four years old, boating off Long Island with Nonno David and Nonna Giulia.

Adriatic-Style Grilled Shrimp

Time from start to finish: 1 hour

The aroma of grilled seafood lightly coated with a mixture of bread crumbs, garlic, and parsley always takes me back to my mother's hometown, Cesenatico, where a mixed grill might include tender baby cuttlefish, squid, shrimp, and scampi—that delicate sweet langoustine we unfortunately don't have here in the States. I can think of no better way to grill shrimp. They are crispy on the outside and moist and sweet inside.

1½ pounds extra-large shrimp

1 small clove garlic

3 to 4 sprigs flat-leaf Italian parsley

Salt

Freshly ground black pepper

⅓ cup extra-virgin olive oil

½ cup fine, dry plain bread crumbs

2 tablespoons freshly squeezed lemon juice

Skewers for grilling

SERVES 4

1. Shell and devein the shrimp.

2. Peel and finely chop the garlic. Finely chop enough parsley leaves to measure 1 tablespoon. Place the shrimp in a large, shallow bowl with the garlic and parsley. Season with salt and pepper. Add the olive oil and bread crumbs a little at a time until the shrimp are lightly coated with the mixture. There should be just enough bread crumbs to allow the marinade to cling to the shrimp but not so much that they form a thick crust, and only as much olive oil as the crumbs will absorb. Let the shrimp marinate for 30 minutes.

3. Preheat a charcoal or gas grill until it is very hot.

4. Thread the shrimp onto the skewers. Cook the shrimp until pink, about 2 minutes on each side. After turning the skewers, sprinkle with the lemon juice. Serve at once.

Pan–Roasted Pompano

Time from start to finish: 15 minutes

3 tablespoons butter

4 pompano fillets (1½ to 2 pounds), skin on

Salt

Freshly ground black pepper

¼ cup freshly squeezed lemon juice

My paternal grandparents used to have a condo in Hallandale, Florida, and sometimes my parents and I would stay there as a welcome getaway from cold New York winters. I remember we would go to the dock to meet the fishing boats that would sell the fish that had been caught by hotel-bound tourists. It was during these Florida escapes that I became enamored of the sweet, melt-in-your-mouth flesh of pompano. My mother cooked it in an arguably un-Italian but nonetheless delectable style, pan roasting it with butter and lemon. Seafood in Italy is almost always cooked in olive oil rather than butter, but if they had pompano in Italy, I think it would create an exception to that rule.

SERVES 4

1. Put the butter in a nonstick skillet large enough to accommodate all the fish, or divide the butter in half between two smaller skillets, and place over medium–high heat. When the butter foam begins to subside and the butter just begins to darken, put the fish fillets in, skin side up. When the fish is lightly browned, after 3 to 4 minutes, turn the fillets over. Season with salt and pepper, add the lemon juice, and cover the pan. Continue cooking until the fish flakes easily when prodded with a fork, 4 to 5 minutes.

2. When the fish is done, the liquid in the pan should be a sauce thick enough to coat a spoon. If there is still too much liquid, raise the heat to high until it has reduced. If the pan is too dry, add a little water, loosen the cooking residue on the pan bottom, and let the sauce reduce. When the sauce is ready, turn the fish so the flesh side is well coated, then transfer it to a serving platter and pour the sauce over it. Serve at once.

Shrimp with Olive Oil and Lemon

Time from start to finish: 20 minutes

1 tablespoon red wine vinegar

Salt

2 pounds large (16 to 20 per pound) shrimp, in the shell

4 tablespoons extra-virgin olive oil

2 tablespoons freshly squeezed lemon juice

When my parents and I would vacation in Florida during the winter, we would look for places that sold live shrimp for bait. We didn't use the shrimp for fishing, though; we took them back to the condo we were staying at and cooked them! Now that I live in Florida, when I come across fresh Key West shrimp (often from the back of a truck parked on the side of the road), this is how I make them. When shrimp are really fresh, this is one of my favorite ways to prepare them because the flavor is pure shrimp. When using larger shrimp, I like to cut them in half lengthwise, so that there is more surface area to coat with the olive oil and lemon. A trick I learned from my mother is to add a splash of vinegar when boiling seafood. This highlights its sweet, fresh flavor.

SERVES 4 AS AN APPETIZER

1. Fill a pot with 4 quarts water, place over high heat, and bring to a boil. Add the vinegar, 1 tablespoon salt, and the shrimp. Cover the pot to bring the water back to a boil as quickly as possible. The shrimp will be done as soon as they are pink through and through, less than 1 minute after the water comes back to a boil. Drain them.

2. As soon as the shrimp are cool enough to handle, remove the shells and cut the shrimp in half lengthwise. Devein the shrimp and place them in a serving bowl. Season lightly with salt, add the olive oil and lemon juice, and toss well. Serve warm or at room temperature, with some good crusty bread.

My wife and daughters in
Portofino, Italy.

Chapter 4:

Dolci: Desserts

I've never really had a sweet tooth. I do love chocolate, and pastries are my favorite breakfast, but if I had to choose between a dish of pasta and a dessert, the pasta would likely prevail. My grandmother Nonna Mary, on the other hand, did love sweets. For her birthday, she would just as soon skip the meal and focus on dessert instead. Ironically, she did not do a lot of baking; in fact, no one in my family does, with the exception of my wife and daughters. One thing Nonna Mary did bake, though, was *ciambella*, a sweet breakfast bread that she always seemed to have on hand. And although my Nonna Giulia did not bake often, her baklavà was legendary. My mother is not really a baker either, but that doesn't mean she didn't make desserts when I was growing up. Her chocolate mousse and *diplomatico* are two that I remember very fondly and continue to make to this day. Having a gelato in the afternoon is a ritual I still enjoy when I'm in Italy, as does my family. I've discovered how easy it is to make homemade ice cream; we've invested in an ice-cream maker and now often make ice cream at home.

Chiacchere della Nonna

Time from start to finish: 30 minutes

2 tablespoons unsalted butter

1¼ cups all-purpose flour, plus extra for dusting

2 tablespoons sugar

1 tablespoon whole milk

1 tablespoon dry white wine

¼ teaspoon salt

Vegetable oil

2 tablespoons confectioners' sugar

Nonna Mary, my mother's mother, was an expert at frying, and it was always a treat for me when she made this fried dough topped with powdered sugar. She called them *chiacchere della Nonna*, which means "Grandma's chatter." They are also sometimes known as *frappe*. My mother would also occasionally make them, though not often enough. This is an adaptation of her recipe. Although they are at their absolute best when eaten hot, they are also very good at room temperature several hours after they've been fried.

MAKES ABOUT 12 *CHIACCHERE*

1. Cut the butter into 4 pieces and put it with the flour, sugar, milk, white wine, and salt in a food processor. Run the processor until a dough forms. Remove the dough and wrap it in plastic. Let it rest for at least 15 minutes.

2. Dust a large cutting board with flour. Remove the plastic wrap, flatten the dough with your hands, and place it on the board. Sprinkle some flour over the dough and roll it out about ⅛ inch thick. Use a fluted pastry wheel to cut ½-inch-wide strips. Strips that are 6 inches or longer can be looped into a loose knot. Shorter strips can be left as they are.

3. Pour enough oil into a skillet to come ½ inch up the sides and place over medium-high heat. Test the oil with a corner of one of the strips; when it makes the oil sizzle, the oil is hot enough. Carefully slip as many pieces into the skillet as will fit comfortably. As soon as they are brown on the bottom, turn them over. Brown the other side, then transfer them to a platter lined with paper towels. They will only need to fry for about 1 minute on each side. Continue until all the strips are done. Use a small fine-mesh strainer to sprinkle them generously with the confectioners' sugar and serve hot or at room temperature.

Baklavà

Time from start to finish: 1 hour, plus time to let the baklavà cool

My paternal grandmother, Nonna Giulia, was famous for her baklavà. Unfortunately, that recipe was never written down, and since baklavà is not one of my father's favorite desserts, I don't remember my mother ever making it. When I met my wife, Lael, I discovered desserts are her specialty, which works out perfectly, since I much prefer cooking to baking. One of the things she makes is a baklavà that reminds me of Nonna Giulia's. I particularly like the balance of salty and sweet that salted pistachios gives it.

MAKES ABOUT 30 PIECES

PASTRY

1. Preheat the oven to 400°F on the regular bake setting.

2. Coarsely chop the almonds and pistachios. You can do this in a food processor, but be careful not to pulverize the nuts. The chopped pieces should be about the size of short-grained rice. Transfer the nuts to a bowl and add the cinnamon and sugar. Mix well.

3. Melt the butter over low heat or in the microwave. Place a sheet of phyllo dough on a baking tray and brush it with some of the melted butter. Place another sheet over it and brush it with butter. Continue until you have a total of 8 sheets of phyllo dough, then sprinkle half of the nut mixture over the top layer. Cover with 5 more sheets of buttered phyllo dough, then sprinkle three-quarters of the remaining nut mixture on top. Add the remaining sheets of buttered phyllo dough, then cover with the remaining nut mixture. Cut the stack into 3-inch squares, then cut each square diagonally to form triangles.

4. Bake for 10 minutes. Reduce the heat to 350°F and bake for 15 minutes more.

SYRUP AND SERVING

1. While the baklavà is baking, put all the ingredients for the syrup into a 1-quart saucepan over medium-low heat. Once the liquid begins to bubble, simmer for 10 minutes more. Remove from the heat.

2. When the baklavà is out of the oven, let it rest for 10 minutes, then brush the syrup over it. Serve at room temperature or chilled.

FOR THE PASTRY

1 cup blanched almonds

½ cup roasted salted pistachios, shelled

½ teaspoon cinnamon

2 tablespoons sugar

8 tablespoons (1 stick) unsalted butter

½ pound phyllo dough

FOR THE SYRUP

¾ cup sugar

¾ cup water

1 teaspoon honey

½ teaspoon orange extract

1 teaspoon freshly squeezed lemon juice

Chocolate Mousse

Time from start to finish: 12 hours

8 ounces semisweet chocolate

6 eggs

2 tablespoons sugar

1 tablespoon rum (optional)

We are a chocolate-loving family. From my father I learned how to slowly let a piece of fine dark chocolate melt in my mouth, allowing the luscious flavor to fill my palate. As a child, I remember what a joyous occasion it was when my mother would make this chocolate mousse. She would let me do most of it myself, and I remember how she taught me to carefully fold the egg whites to preserve the air we had whipped into them. Our kids like making this too, and they even help with cleanup—at least by licking the bowl! I like making it with rum, and at a fraction of a tablespoon per portion, the alcohol is not really an issue, but some kids may prefer the flavor without it.

SERVES 8

1. Place a saucepan filled halfway with water over medium heat. Cut the chocolate into small pieces and put it in a small metal bowl that will fit over the saucepan. Place the bowl over the saucepan. Once the chocolate has melted, reduce the heat to the lowest setting.

2. While the chocolate is melting, separate the eggs, placing the yolks in one mixing bowl and the whites in another. Be very careful not to get any of the yolk in the bowl with the whites. Add the sugar to the yolks and whip at high speed until the yolks turn pale and form ribbons. Mix in the rum, if using. Add the melted chocolate and mix thoroughly.

3. Whip the egg whites until they form soft peaks. If using the same whisk that was used for beating the yolks, make sure to clean it thoroughly beforehand. Carefully fold the whites into the chocolate mixture. Once you obtain a homogeneous mixture, pour the mousse into 8 serving cups or goblets. Refrigerate, covered, overnight before serving.

La Sbrisolona

Time from start to finish: 1 hour and 10 minutes

Sbrisolona is actually a dialect word that corresponds to *sbriciolona* in Italian, which in turn means "crumbly." And that describes this cake perfectly, because it is made from crumbly dough that is baked together. When it is served, it is broken into irregular pieces and sometimes dunked in grappa or sweet wine. For breakfast, it's great dunked into your *caffèlatte*. It originated in Mantova, but it is also made in Emilia-Romagna, and in Verona, where our cooking school is located.

8 tablespoons (1 stick) unsalted butter, plus extra for the pan

4 ounces blanched almonds

½ cup sugar

1½ cups all-purpose flour

⅔ cup yellow cornmeal

Grated zest of 1 lemon

2 egg yolks

SERVES 8

1. Cut the butter into 12 pieces and let it sit at room temperature for about 15 minutes.

2. Preheat the oven to 375°F on the regular bake setting.

3. Put the almonds and sugar in a food processor and chop very finely. Transfer to a mixing bowl, add the flour and cornmeal, and mix well. Add the lemon zest and egg yolks to the bowl and work the mixture with your hands until it forms little pellets. Add the butter, working it in with your fingers until it is completely incorporated, forming a crumbly dough.

4. Smear the bottom of a 10- to 12-inch round cake pan with butter and crumble the dough into the pan until it is uniformly distributed. Place the pan on the upper rack of the oven and bake for 40 minutes, until the top turns a nutty brown color. Cool before serving.

Diplomatico

Time from start to finish: 12 hours

3 tablespoons sugar

½ cup Italian coffee, hot

½ cup water

2 tablespoons rum

8 ounces semisweet chocolate

1 (12 ounce) store-bought pound cake

6 large eggs

1 cup heavy cream

1 cup assorted fresh berries (such as strawberries, blackberries, blueberries, and raspberries)

My earliest memories of helping my mother in the kitchen are of stirring risotto and helping to make this dessert. My mother still makes it, and we also make it at our house. At our cooking school in Italy, we end each course with it. We encourage our students to unleash their creativity in decorating it, and we have assembled an impressive collection of photos of their creations.

SERVES 8

1. In a small bowl, mix 1 tablespoon of the sugar into the coffee and stir to dissolve. Add the water and rum and set aside to cool.

2. Place a saucepan filled halfway with water over medium heat. Cut the chocolate into small pieces and put it in a small metal bowl that will fit over the saucepan. Place the bowl over the saucepan. Once the chocolate has melted, reduce the heat to the lowest setting.

3. Cut the pound cake into ¼-inch-thick slices. Line the bottom and sides of a 1½-quart loaf pan with the slices. Using a pastry brush, generously dab the pound cake with some of the rum-and-coffee mixture. The cake should be soaked through but not so drenched that the liquid oozes out.

4. Separate the eggs, placing the yolks in one mixing bowl and the whites in another. Be very careful not to get any of the yolk in the bowl with the whites. Add the remaining 2 tablespoons sugar to the yolks and whip at high speed until the yolks turn pale and form ribbons. Add the melted chocolate and mix well. Whip the egg whites on high speed until they form stiff peaks. If using the same whisk that was used for beating the yolks, make sure to clean it thoroughly beforehand. Carefully fold the whites into the chocolate mixture. To make folding easier, you can mix in a spoonful of egg whites first to soften the mixture.

5. Pour the mixture into the lined loaf pan. Cover with a layer of the remaining sliced pound cake and use the pastry brush to soak it with the rum-and-coffee mixture. Cover with plastic and refrigerate overnight or up to 2 days.

6. When ready to serve, whip the cream until it forms stiff peaks. Unmold the cake onto a flat plate, tapping it gently to loosen it. Frost it with the whipped cream and decorate with the berries. Serve chilled.

Nonna Mary's *Ciambella*

Time from start to finish: 50 minutes

When I was growing up in New York, from third grade through high school, I was blessed with the opportunity to spend my summers in Italy. I would stay with my grandmother in Cesenatico, hang out at the beach with my friends, and eat the wonderful food my grandmother cooked. I have never become accustomed to the traditional American breakfast of eggs and fried pork products, or even cereal. Some fresh bread with butter and jam and *caffèlatte* is my preferred breakfast, with the proportion of coffee to milk increasing as I have gotten older, from just a drop in a large cup of milk when I was little, to mostly coffee with a splash of milk as an adult. But even better than bread and butter is a breakfast sweet such as my grandmother's *ciambella*. She always seemed to have some on hand. It's very easy to make and keeps wonderfully on the kitchen counter for as long as a week. It may well keep even longer, but I've never been able to resist eating it for long enough to find out. The classic shape of a *ciambella* is a ring; in fact, there is a saying for when something doesn't work out: *non tutte le ciambelle riescono col buco*, which means, "not all *ciambelle* come out with a hole." My grandmother always made hers in the shape of a loaf—it was no less delicious for it, and that is how I still prefer to make it.

3 cups all-purpose flour

¾ cup sugar

2 tablespoons whole milk

2 eggs

1 tablespoon baking powder

¼ teaspoon salt

12 tablespoons (1½ sticks) unsalted butter

Grated zest of 1 lemon

1 egg yolk

SERVES 8

1. Preheat the oven to 375°F on the regular bake setting

2. Put the flour, sugar, milk, and 2 eggs in the bowl of a food processor. Add the baking powder and salt, taking care not to put one on top of the other or the salt may inhibit the action of the baking powder. Cut the butter into at least a dozen pieces. Add the butter and lemon zest to the other ingredients and pulse until a dough forms.

3. Transfer the dough to a counter and knead it gently until you obtain a smooth ball. Shape the dough into a loaf about 12 inches long and 3 inches wide. Place it on a baking sheet that has been buttered and floured or lined with a nonstick baking mat. Place the egg yolk in a small bowl. Add 2 teaspoons water, and whisk. Make 4 or 5 shallow diagonal cuts on top of the dough and brush the surface with the yolk mixture.

4. Bake for 35 minutes. The *ciambella* is ready when it is golden brown and feels fairly firm when prodded.

Polenta Cookies

Time from start to finish: at least 1 hour and 45 minutes, plus time for cooling

2 cups finely ground yellow cornmeal

1 cup all-purpose flour

1¼ cups confectioners' sugar

2 large eggs

12 tablespoons (1½ sticks) unsalted butter

⅛ teaspoon salt

1 teaspoon baking powder

Grated zest of 1 lemon

I first met the Simili sisters when I was still a teenager. That first encounter was at their father's award-winning bakery in Bologna. I remember I was astounded at how fast they were and how many things they managed to do at one time. When my parents brought me into the store to meet them, Valeria was at the counter. She made me feel like meeting me was one of the most wonderful things in the world, while simultaneously serving at least three customers. Margherita was at the cash register; she managed to make me feel the same way, all the while ringing up, providing change to, and enquiring about the families of at least three customers. Margherita's record for the number of tortellini she is able to shape into a perfect bishop's hat in one minute is forty-three. They worked grueling hours, and Margherita would joke about how she would catch up on sleep in the car at red lights. They assisted my mother when she opened her cooking school in Bologna and occasionally taught some of their amazing baked delicacies. Thirty-five years later, they are still good friends, and though they are older than I am, they still have more energy. They have become world-renowned teachers, sought after in Italy, the United States, Japan, and beyond. These cookies that I learned from them are as delicious as any of their creations, yet easy enough for a nonbaker like me. In Italian they are called *gialletti*, because of the golden color they get from the yellow cornmeal that is their principal ingredient.

MAKES APPROXIMATELY 30 (2½-INCH SQUARE) COOKIES

1. Place the cornmeal, flour, confectioners' sugar, and eggs in the bowl of a food processor. Cut the butter into small pieces and add to the other ingredients. Add the salt and the baking powder, being careful not to put one on top of the other, as salt can inhibit the action of baking powder. Add the lemon zest to the bowl. Run the processor until you obtain a smooth, homogeneous dough. Remove the dough, wrap it in plastic, and place it in the refrigerator for at least 1 hour. Do not be concerned if the dough feels soft and sticky. It will firm up once it has chilled.

2. Preheat the oven to 350°F on the regular bake setting.

3. Unwrap the dough, cut it in half, rewrap one half in the plastic, and put it back in the refrigerator. Put the other half on a counter, preferably a cool surface such as granite, marble, or stainless steel. Flatten it a bit with your hands, then use a rolling pin to roll it out until it is ¼ inch thick. Cut the dough into whatever shapes you like (I find squares easiest to deal with) and place them on a cookie sheet that has been buttered and floured or lined with a nonstick baking mat. Collect the trimmings into a ball, wrap in plastic, and place in the refrigerator. Take out the half of the dough still in the refrigerator and repeat the process. Continue until all the dough has been used.

4. Bake for about 15 minutes, until the cookies begin to brown around the edges. Let cool completely before serving.

At four years old, learning to ride a bicycle in Cesenatico.

Crema Bruciata

Time from start to finish: 26 hours

1⅓ cups heavy cream

½ cup whole milk

4 egg yolks

⅓ cup sugar, plus 4 teaspoons for the topping

¼ cup Italian coffee

On an idyllic spot in the heart of the medieval town of Sirmione, with a terrace overlooking Lake Garda, is Ristorante Signori, where we take our students on the last day of our cooking course in Italy. We have been going there since we opened our school in 2000 so that our students can taste the flavors of the extraordinary freshwater fish from Italy's largest lake. The finale is an exquisite *crema bruciata*, which is the Italian equivalent of crème brûlée. It is a coffee-flavored, smooth-as-silk, heavenly dessert that my wife and I look forward to every time we go there. Finally, after many years, the chef agreed to give me his recipe. I am perfectly happy to eat it without the burnt-sugar topping; in fact, I even prefer it that way. But to make it the way it was intended, you'll need a culinary blowtorch, which is easily obtainable in most kitchen-supply stores and rather fun to use. I tried just using my broiler, but by the time the sugar browns, the custard has heated too much and loses some of its fine, silky texture.

SERVES 4

1. Preheat the oven to 325°F on the regular bake setting.

2. Put the cream and milk in a 1- to 2-quart saucepan over medium heat. Once steam is released when the liquid is stirred, remove from the heat.

3. Put the egg yolks and ⅓ cup sugar in a bowl and whip with an electric mixer until pale yellow and custardlike in consistency. Slowly add the warm milk and cream while whisking on low speed. Mix in the coffee and transfer to 4 individual-size ovenproof ramekins. Place them in a baking dish and pour enough water in the baking dish to come halfway up the sides of the ramekins, being careful not to splash any water into the custard. Place the baking dish in the oven and cook for 40 minutes. When ready, the custard should jiggle only slightly when moved. Remove the ramekins from the water bath, and once they are cool, place them in the refrigerator for 24 hours.

4. After 24 hours, sprinkle each custard with a teaspoon of sugar, using a fine-mesh strainer or sifter to distribute it evenly. Ignite the blowtorch and move the flame back and forth over the sugar until it has browned evenly. Place the ramekins back in the refrigerator and chill completely before serving.

Italian Mint Chip Ice Cream

Time from start to finish: 1 hour and 15 minutes

Cioccomenta, as it is called in Italy, seems to be a favorite flavor for everyone in our family—except me. Having managed to grow a healthy mint bush in our backyard, I decided to try making it at home. When I started writing recipes for gelati several years ago, I decided the purchase of an ice-cream maker with a built-in compressor was justified. (I have mastered the art of rationalization.) We've been making ice cream at home ever since. With few exceptions, homemade ice cream is one of the easiest desserts to create, and a relatively inexpensive ice-cream maker with a removable cylinder you keep in the freezer will also work very well. Italian ice cream is characteristically lighter than its American counterpart because milk is usually used instead of cream. No eggs are called for in this recipe, so I use equal parts milk and cream.

2 cups whole milk

2 cups heavy cream

½ cup sugar

1 cup loosely packed fresh mint leaves

2 ounces semisweet chocolate

MAKES 1 GENEROUS QUART

1. Place the milk, cream, sugar, and mint leaves in a saucepan over medium heat. Once the milk is hot enough to release steam when stirred, reduce the heat to low and cook, stirring often, for 5 minutes. Remove from the heat and allow to cool completely.

2. Remove and discard the mint leaves. Use a knife to coarsely chop the chocolate. Stir it into the mixture and freeze in an ice-cream maker according to the manufacturer's instructions. Serve right away or store, tightly covered, in the freezer. It should keep for several days before ice crystals begin to form.

Strawberry Gelato

Time from start to finish: 40 minutes

¾ pound fresh strawberries

¾ cup sugar

¾ cup water

2 tablespoons freshly squeezed
lemon juice

⅓ cup heavy cream

My mother used to teach strawberry ice cream at my parents' cooking school in Bologna. I remember they would always serve it along with Recioto, a wonderful dessert wine from Valpolicella made with dried grapes. It was a fantastic and unexpected pairing, and I always looked forward to it. Ironically, my wife and I now run a cooking school in Valpolicella in collaboration with one of the top producers of Recioto, Marilisa Allegrini. As I was trying out recipes for my previous books, I made several variations of that ice cream—with cantaloupe, with peaches, and with pineapple. But I hadn't made the strawberry ice cream for quite a long time, until we recently took our two girls strawberry picking at a local farm. In no time at all, we had accumulated seventeen pounds of strawberries. When we got home and had finally filled our bellies with the luscious, sweet berries, I froze the remaining ones. (The best way to freeze them, by the way, is to lay them out in a single layer on cookie trays so they don't touch. Once they are frozen, you can store them in zip-top bags.) So what to do with all our frozen strawberries? Ice cream, of course! I tweaked my mother's recipe a bit, adding a bit of lemon juice, which I've found really brightens the fruit flavor. After making a few batches of ice cream, I decided to try something different and came up with the peach-and-strawberry *semifreddo* in the recipe that follows.

MAKES 1 GENEROUS QUART

1. Remove the green tops of the strawberries and rinse them in cold water.

2. Place the berries and the sugar in a food processor and blend until puréed. Add the water and lemon juice and continue blending until all the ingredients are mixed together thoroughly.

3. Whip the cream with a whisk until it begins to thicken and acquires the consistency of yogurt. Add the puréed strawberries and mix thoroughly.

4. Pour the mixture into an ice-cream maker and freeze according to the manufacturer's directions. Serve right away or store, tightly covered, in the freezer. It should keep for several days before ice crystals begin to form.

Peach-and-Strawberry *Semifreddo*

Time from start to finish: 12 hours

In this *semifreddo*, peaches and strawberries taste and look great together. The recipe can easily be adapted to other fruits as well. Peaches and kiwi or mango and strawberries would also pair wonderfully. To make a straight dividing line between the strawberry and the peach layers, freeze the bottom layer until firm, about six hours, before adding the top layer. If you pour in the top layer without freezing the bottom first, the two won't mix, but you'll get a bell-shaped curve as the top sinks in a bit—which I think is actually quite attractive.

1 pound strawberries

1¼ cups sugar

4 tablespoons freshly squeezed lemon juice

1 pound peaches

1 cup heavy cream

2 egg whites

SERVES 8 TO 10

1. Remove the green tops of the strawberries. Quarter the strawberries and place them in a saucepan with ½ cup of the sugar and 2 tablespoons of the lemon juice over medium-low heat. Once the fruit begins bubbling, cover the pan and cook for 10 minutes. Allow to cool completely.

2. Peel and pit the peaches, and cut into ¼-inch slices. Place them in a second saucepan with ½ cup of the sugar and the remaining 2 tablespoons lemon juice. Repeat the cooking procedure in step 1.

3. Once the strawberries and peaches have both cooled, whip the heavy cream together with the remaining ¼ cup sugar until stiff peaks form. Divide the whipped cream into two mixing bowls. Put the cooked strawberries, along with any liquid they have released, in a food processor and puree them. Add the strawberry puree to one of the bowls with the whipped cream and fold together until you obtain a homogeneous mixture. Repeat the same procedure with the cooked peaches, folding them into the cream in the second bowl.

4. Whip the egg whites until soft peaks form. Divide the whites evenly between the two bowls and carefully fold them into the mixtures.

5. Line a 1½-quart loaf pan with plastic wrap and pour in whichever fruit mixture you would like to end up on top of the finished *semifreddo*. Pour in the second fruit mixture (or freeze the bottom layer first to obtain a straight line division between the two; see above). Cover and place in the freezer for at least 10 hours, or overnight.

6. When ready to serve, unmold the *semifreddo* onto a platter or cutting board and slice into portions. If the *semifreddo* does not loosen from the loaf pan easily, wet a towel with very hot water and wipe the bottom and sides of the loaf pan.

Nutella Ice Cream

Time from start to finish: 2 hours

2 cups whole milk

4 egg yolks

⅓ cup sugar

4 ounces (¼ cup) Nutella

Our kids have a love affair with Nutella, as most Italian kids do. Nutella is a sumptuous chocolate-hazelnut spread that has been satisfying Italian kids' afternoon hunger attacks for decades. I remember it as one of my favorite *merende*, or afternoon snacks. It is one of the flavors you often find in the *gelaterie* that proclaim *"Produzione Nostra"*—"Our Own Production." When my wife discovered the existence of World Nutella Day (it's February 5th), our kids decided we needed to celebrate it by re-creating the Nutella ice cream they remembered from Italy.

MAKES 1 QUART

1. Put the milk in a saucepan over medium heat. When the milk is hot enough to release steam when stirred, but not boiling, remove from the heat and pour the hot milk into a heatproof pitcher or cup with a spout.

2. While the milk is heating, put the yolks in a mixing bowl. Add the sugar and whip at high speed until the mixture is pale yellow, thick, and creamy.

3. Slowly add the hot milk to the egg mixture while whisking on low speed. Once half the milk is added, you can begin to pour a little faster until all the milk is added. Add the Nutella and whip on medium speed until it is evenly incorporated.

4. Chill the mixture in the refrigerator. When it is cold, freeze in an ice-cream maker according to the manufacturer's instructions. Serve right away or store, tightly covered, in the freezer. It should keep for several days before ice crystals begin to form.

I am eighteen months old with
Nonna Mary in Cesenatico.

Conversion Charts

Weight Equivalents

The metric weights given in this chart are not exact equivalents, but have been rounded up or down slightly to make measuring easier.

AVOIRDUPOIS	METRIC
¼ ounce	7 grams
½ ounce	15 grams
1 ounce	30 grams
2 ounces	60 grams
3 ounces	90 grams
4 ounces	115 grams
5 ounces	150 grams
6 ounces	175 grams
7 ounces	200 grams
8 ounces (½ pound)	225 grams
9 ounces	250 grams
10 ounces	300 grams
11 ounces	325 grams
12 ounces	350 grams
13 ounces	375 grams
14 ounces	400 grams
15 ounces	425 grams
16 ounces (1 pound)	450 grams
1½ pounds	750 grams
2 pounds	900 grams
2¼ pounds	1 kilogram
3 pounds	1.4 kilograms
4 pounds	1.8 kilograms

Volume Equivalents

These are not exact equivalents for American cups and spoons, but have been rounded up or down slightly to make measuring easier.

AMERICAN	METRIC	IMPERIAL
¼ teaspoon	1.2 milliliters	—
½ teaspoon	2.5 milliliters	—
1 teaspoon	5.0 milliliters	—
½ tablespoon (1½ teaspoons)	7.5 milliliters	—
1 tablespoon (3 teaspoons)	15 milliliters	—
¼ cup (4 tablespoons)	60 milliliters	2 fluid ounces
⅓ cup (5 tablespoons)	75 milliliters	2½ fluid ounces
½ cup (8 tablespoons)	125 milliliters	4 fluid ounces
⅔ cup (10 tablespoons)	150 milliliters	5 fluid ounces
¾ cup (12 tablespoons)	175 milliliters	6 fluid ounces
1 cup (16 tablespoons)	250 milliliters	8 fluid ounces
1¼ cups	300 milliliters	10 fluid ounces (½ pint)
1½ cups	350 milliliters	12 fluid ounces
2 cups (1 pint)	500 milliliters	16 fluid ounces
2½ cups	625 milliliters	20 fluid ounces (1 pint)
1 quart	1 liter	32 fluid ounces

Oven Temperature Equivalents

OVEN MARK	°F	°C	GAS
very cool	250–275	130–140	½–1
cool	300	150	2
warm	325	170	3
moderate	350	180	4
moderately hot	375–400	190–200	5–6
hot	425–450	220–230	7–8
very hot	475	250	9

Index

Page numbers in italics refer to images.

A

Adriatic-style grilled shrimp, 141
Almonds:
  baklavà, *150*, 151
  la sbrisolona, 153
Anchovy(ies):
  pizza topping, 21
  Roman-style chicory salad, 36
Animelle croccanti (Giuliano's crisp
  sweetbreads), 133
Apricots: grilled fruit, 54
Artichokes, frittata with, 24–25
Asparagus fritters, 37

B

Baklavà, *150*, 151
Bananas: grilled fruit, 54
Basil: risotto with pesto, 98, *99*
Beans. *See* cannellini beans; green beans
Béchamel sauce, 77
Beef:
  boeuf Giuliano, 116
  Bolognese meat sauce, 76
  homemade meat broth, 60
  Lael's meatloaf, 117
  mahshi, 126–27
  meatballs with tomatoes and peas, 118–19
  stuffed zucchini, 128, *129*
  tagliata with garlic and parsley, 120, *121*
Beets: insalata Russa, *30*, 31–32
Belgian endive:
  and radicchio, grilled, 52
  salad, Roman-style, 36
Bell peppers. *See* peppers
Berries:
  diplomatico, 154, *155*
  peach-and-strawberry *semifreddo*,
    164, 165
  strawberry gelato, 162, *163*
Black truffles, veal scaloppine with, 125
Boeuf Giuliano, 116
Bolognese lasagne, 78–80, *79*
Bolognese meat sauce, 76
Borekitas, 22–23
Bread crumbs:
  baked tomatoes, *38*, 39
  passatelli, 64, *65*
Brodetto, my version, *138*, 139–40
Broth, meat, homemade, 60
Brussels sprouts braised with pancetta,
  42, *43*
Butter, tomato, and onion sauce, my mother's,
  72

C

Cabbage:
  mahshi, 126–27
  minestrone, 61
  Piedmontese Savoy cabbage and bean
    soup, 69
Cakes:
  diplomatico, 154, *155*
  Nonna Mary's *ciambella*, 156, 157
  la sbrisolona, 153
Cannellini beans:
  minestrone, 61
  Nonno Fin's, 45
  Piedmontese Savoy cabbage and bean
    soup, 69
  tuna, bean, and red onion salad, 34, *35*
Capers, chicken breasts with tomatoes, olives,
  and, 108, *109*
Carrots: insalata russa, *30*, 31–32

Cauliflower soup, 59
Cheese. *See also* Prosciutto; *specific types*
    filling, *borekitas* with, 22–23
    ham-and-cheese *crespelle*, 90, *91*
    Italian "mac and cheese," 86
Chiacchere della Nonna, 148, *149*
Chicken:
    breasts, grilled marinated, 107
    breasts, with tomatoes, capers, and olives,
        108, *109*
    homemade meat broth, 60
    with a lemon inside, 106
    photo-shoot chicken, *110*, 111–12
Chickpeas, spinach and, 47
Chicory salad, Roman-style, 36
Chocolate:
    diplomatico, 154, *155*
    Italian mint chip ice cream, 161
    mousse, 152
    Nutella ice cream, 166
Ciambella, Nonna Mary's, *156*, 157
Claiborne, Craig, 123
Coffee:
    crema bruciata, 160
    diplomatico, 154, *155*
Cookies, polenta, 158–59
Cornmeal:
    polenta cookies, 158–59
    la sbrisolona, 153
Crema bruciata, 160
Crespelle, ham-and-cheese, 90, *91*
Crisp sweetbreads, Giuliano's, 133
Custard: *crema bruciata*, 160

D
Desserts, 17
    baklavà, *150*, 151

chiacchere della Nonna, 148, *149*
chocolate mousse, 152
crema bruciata, 160
diplomatico, 154, *155*
Italian mint chip ice cream, 161
Nonna Mary's *ciambella*, *156*, 157
Nutella ice cream, 166
peach-and-strawberry *semifreddo*,
    164, 165
polenta cookies, 158–59
la sbrisolona, 153
strawberry gelato, 162, *163*
Diplomatico, 154, *155*

E
Egg pasta of Emilia-Romagna, 70–71
Eggplant:
    grilled, 53
    risotto with, 95
Eggs. *See* frittata
Endive. *See* Belgian endive

F
Farfalle with sausage and peas, *84*, 85
Fettuccine with orange, 87
Figs: grilled fruit, 54
Fish:
    il brodetto, my version, *138*, 139–40
    fried seafood *alla Romagnola*, 134–35
    pan-roasted pompano, 142, *143*
Fontina, Piedmontese rice and, 94
Frappe, 148
Fried foods:
    asparagus fritters, 37
    chiacchere della Nonna, 148, *149*
    fried Parmesan cheese–battered lamb
        chops, 114, *115*

fried seafood *alla Romagnola*, 134–35
fried zucchini blossoms, 44
potato fritters, 49
Frittata:
with artichokes, 24–25
with pancetta and potatoes, 26–27
with zucchini, 28
Fritters. *See* fried foods
Fruit, grilled, 54
Fusilli with peppers and pancetta, *88*, 89

G

Garlic and parsley, tagliata with, 120, *121*
Gelato, strawberry, 162, *163*
Giuliano's crisp sweetbreads, 133
Green beans:
insalata russa, *30*, 31–32
minestrone, 61
stewed with tomatoes, 46
Grilling, 50–55
Adriatic-style grilled shrimp, 141
grilled Belgian endive and radicchio, 52
grilled eggplant, 53
grilled fruit, 54
grilled marinated chicken breasts, 107
grilled onions, 51
grilled portobello mushrooms, 52
grilled sea scallops with a parsley-thyme
sauce, 136, *137*
grilled zucchini, 53
roasted peppers, 51
tagliata with garlic and parsley, 120, *121*

H

Ham. *See also* Prosciutto
ham-and-cheese *crespelle*, 90, *91*
Hazelnuts: Nutella ice cream, 166

Homemade mayonnaise, 29
Homemade meat broth, 60

I

Ice cream:
Italian mint chip, 161
Nutella, 166
strawberry gelato, 162, *163*
Insalata mista, 33
Insalata russa, *30*, 31–32
Italian baby back ribs, *130*, 131
Italian latkes, 48
Italian "mac and cheese," 86
Italian mint chip ice cream, 161

L

Lamb:
braised with peppers, 113
fried Parmesan cheese–battered, 114, *115*
mahshi, 126–27
Lasagne, Bolognese, 78–80, *79*
Latkes, Italian, 48
Leeks and peas, braised, 40
Lemon:
chicken with a lemon inside, 106
shrimp with olive oil and, 144
Lobster: *il brodetto*, my version, *138*, 139–40

M

"Mac and cheese," Italian, 86
Maccheroni soup with sausage and porcini,
66, 67–68
Mahshi, 126–27
Margherita pizza topping, 20
Mayonnaise, homemade, 29
Meat broth, homemade, 60
Meat sauce, Bolognese, 76

Meatballs with tomatoes and peas, 118–19
Meatloaf, Lael's, 117
Minestrone, 61
    with rice, cold, *62*, 63
Mint chip ice cream, Italian, 161
Mousse, chocolate, 152
Mozzarella: classic Margherita pizza topping, 20
Mushrooms:
    maccheroni soup with sausage and
        porcini, *66*, 67–68
    penne with, 81
    portobello, grilled, 52
    risotto with a mushroom medley, *96*, 97
    risotto with fresh tomatoes, peas, and
        porcini, 100
    sautéed mushroom pizza topping, 21
    veal stew with, 132
Mussels: *il brodetto*, my version, *138*, 139–40

N

Neapolitan pizza topping, 21
Nonna Giulia's rice, 92
Nonna Mary's *ciambella*, *156*, 157
Nonna Mary's white rice, 93
Nutella ice cream, 166

O

Okra with fresh tomatoes, 41
Olive oil and lemon, shrimp with, 144
Olives, chicken breasts with tomatoes, capers,
    and, 108, *109*
Onions:
    grilled, 51
    Italian latkes, 48
    my mother's butter, tomato, and onion
        sauce, 72
    tuna, bean, and red onion salad, 34, *35*

Orange, fettuccine with, 87

P

Pancetta:
    Brussels sprouts braised with, 42, *43*
    frittata with potatoes and, 26–27
    fusilli with peppers and, *88*, 89
    Piedmontese Savoy cabbage and bean
        soup, 69
Pappardelle with sausage and peppers, Al
    Cantunzein's, 82, *83*
Parmigiano-Reggiano:
    fried Parmesan cheese–battered lamb
        chops, 114, *115*
    passatelli, 64, *65*
Parsley:
    parsley-thyme sauce, grilled sea scallops
        with, 136, *137*
    tagliata with garlic and, 120, *121*
Passatelli, 64, *65*
Pasta, 70–89
    Bolognese lasagne, 78–80, *79*
    Bolognese meat sauce, 76
    egg pasta of Emilia–Romagna, 70–71
    farfalle with sausage and peas, *84*, 85
    fettuccine with orange, 87
    fusilli with peppers and pancetta, *88*, 89
    Italian "mac and cheese," 86
    maccheroni soup with sausage and
        porcini, *66*, 67–68
    my mother's butter, tomato, and onion
        sauce, 72
    pappardelle with sausage and peppers, Al
        Cantunzein's, 82, *83*
    penne with mushrooms, 81
    Swiss chard tortelloni with tomato sauce,
        73–75, *74*

Pastries. *See* desserts
Peaches:
    grilled fruit, 54
    peach-and-strawberry *semifreddo*,
        164, 165
Peas:
    farfalle with sausage and, *84*, 85
    insalata russa, *30*, 31–32
    and leeks, braised, 40
    meatballs with tomatoes and, 118–19
    risotto with fresh tomatoes, porcini, and,
        100
Penne with mushrooms, 81
Peppers:
    grilled vegetable pizza topping, 20
    lamb braised with, 113
    Nonna Giulia's rice, 92
    and pancetta, fusilli with, *88*, 89
    photo-shoot chicken, *110*, 111–12
    roasted, 51
    sausage and, Al Cantunzein's pappardelle
        with, 82, *83*
Pesto, risotto with, 98, *99*
Photo-shoot chicken, *110*, 111–12
Piedmontese rice and Fontina, 94
Piedmontese Savoy cabbage and bean soup, 69
Pies, savory: *borekitas*, 22–23
Pistachios: baklavà, *150*, 151
Pizza, 17, *18*
    basic recipe, 19
    toppings, 20–21
Plums: grilled fruit, 54
Polenta cookies, 158–59
Pompano, pan-roasted, 142, *143*
Porcini, 97
    maccheroni soup with sausage and, *66*,
        67–68

penne with mushrooms, 81
    risotto with fresh tomatoes, peas, and, 100
Pork. *See also* Ham; Pancetta; Prosciutto;
    Sausage
    Italian baby back ribs, *130*, 131
    Lael's meatloaf, 117
Portobello mushrooms, grilled, 52
Potatoes:
    cauliflower soup with, 59
    frittata with pancetta and, 26–27
    insalata russa, *30*, 31–32
    Italian latkes, 48
    minestrone, 61
    Piedmontese Savoy cabbage and bean soup
        with, 69
    potato fritters, 49
Primi, 17. *See also* Pasta; Rice; Risotto; Soup(s)
Prosciutto:
    pizza topping, 20
    Swiss chard tortelloni with tomato sauce,
        73–75, *74*
    uccellini scappati, *122*, 123
Puntarelle, 36

R

Radicchio and Belgian endive, grilled, 52
Ribs: Italian baby back ribs, *130*, 131
Rice. *See also* Risotto
    mahshi, 126–27
    minestrone with, cold, *62*, 63
    Nonna Giulia's, 92
    Nonna Mary's, 93
    Piedmontese rice and Fontina, 94
    stuffed zucchini, 128, *129*
Risotto, 17
    with a mushroom medley, *96*, 97
    with eggplant, 95

with fresh tomatoes, peas, and porcini, 100

with pesto, 98, *99*

Russian salad, *30*, 31–32

S

Salad(s), 17

chicory, Roman-style, 36

insalata mista, 33

insalata russa (Russian salad), *30*, 31–32

tuna, bean, and red onion, 34, *35*

Sauce(s):

béchamel, 77

Bolognese meat sauce, 76

butter, tomato, and onion, my mother's, 72

homemade mayonnaise, 29

parsley-thyme, grilled sea scallops with, 136, *137*

Sausage:

farfalle with peas and, *84*, 85

maccheroni soup with porcini and, *66*, 67–68

and peppers, Al Cantunzein's pappardelle with, 82, *83*

pizza topping, 20

Savoy cabbage:

and bean soup, Piedmontese, 69

mahshi, 126–27

minestrone, 61

la Sbrisolona, 153

Scallops:

il brodetto, my version, *138*, 139–40

fried seafood *alla Romagnola*, 134–35

grilled, with a parsley-thyme sauce, 136, *137*

Seafood, 134–44. *See also specific types*

il brodetto, my version, *138*, 139–40

fried *alla Romagnola*, 134–35

Secondi, 17. *See also specific meats and seafood*

Semifreddo, peach-and-strawberry, *164*, 165

Shrimp:

il brodetto, my version, *138*, 139–40

fried seafood *alla Romagnola*, 134–35

grilled, Adriatic-style, 141

insalata russa, *30*, 31–32

with olive oil and lemon, 144

Simili, Margherita, 158

Simili, Valeria, 158

Soup(s), 17, 59–69

il brodetto, my version, *138*, 139–40

cauliflower, 59

homemade meat broth, 60

maccheroni, with sausage and porcini, *66*, 67–68

minestrone, 61

minestrone with rice, cold, *62*, 63

passatelli, 64, *65*

Savoy cabbage and bean, Piedmontese, 69

Spinach:

and chickpeas, 47

filling, *borekitas* with, 22–23

green pasta, 70–71

Squash. *See also* Zucchini

blossoms, fried, 44

Squid: fried seafood *alla Romagnola*, 134–35

Steak: tagliata with garlic and parsley, 120, *121*

Stew(s):

boeuf Giuliano, 116

veal, with mushrooms, 132

Strawberries:

peach-and-strawberry *semifreddo*, *164*, 165

strawberry gelato, 162, *163*
Stuffed cabbage (*mahshi*), 126–27
Stuffed zucchini, 128, *129*
Sweetbreads, Giuliano's crisp, 133
Swiss chard tortelloni with tomato sauce,
    73–75, *74*

T

Tagliata with garlic and parsley, 120, *121*
Thyme: parsley-thyme sauce, grilled sea
    scallops with, 136, *137*
Tomato sauce(s):
    Al Cantunzein's pappardelle with sausage
        and peppers, 82, *83*
    Bolognese meat sauce, 76
    my mother's butter, tomato, and onion
        sauce, 72
    Swiss chard tortelloni with, 73–75, *74*
    uccellini scappati with, *122*, 123
Tomatoes:
    baked, *38*, 39
    chicken breasts with capers, olives, and,
        108, *109*
    classic Margherita pizza topping, 20
    fresh, okra with, 41
    fresh, risotto with peas, porcini, and, 100
    green beans stewed with, 46
    Italian baby back ribs, *130*, 131
    maccheroni soup with sausage and
        porcini, *66*, 67–68
    meatballs with peas and, 118–19
    Neapolitan pizza *alla marinara*, 21
    Nonna Giulia's rice, 92
    Nonno Fin's beans with, 45
    photo-shoot chicken, *110*, 111–12
    risotto with eggplant and, 95
    stuffed zucchini, 128, *129*

Tortelloni, Swiss chard, with tomato sauce,
    73–75, *74*
Truffles, black, veal scaloppine with, 125
Tuna, bean, and red onion salad, 34, *35*

U

Uccellini scappati, *122*, 123

V

Veal:
    cutlets, 124
    homemade meat broth, 60
    rolls (*uccellini scappati*), *122*, 123
    scaloppine with black truffles, 125
    stew, with mushrooms, 132
Vegetables. *See also* Salad(s); *specific*
    vegetables
    grilled vegetable pizza topping, 20

W

Wild mushrooms. *See also* Porcini
    risotto with a mushroom medley, *96*, 97

Z

Zucchini:
    blossoms, fried, 44
    frittata with, 28
    grilled, 53
    grilled vegetable pizza topping, 20
    minestrone, 61
    photo-shoot chicken, *110*, 111–12
    stuffed, 128, *129*